WHEN SHMACK HAPPENS

The Making of
a Spiritual Champion

BY AMBER NEBEN

EDITED BY JENNA D. SAMPSON

Published by Neben Px4, LLC

ISBN: 0991303008
ISBN 13: 9780991303007

Published by Neben Px4, LLC: Perseverance, Patience, Perspective, Power

WHEN SHMACK HAPPENS: The Making of a Spiritual Champion
Copyright 2014 by Amber Neben

This title is also available as a Neben Px4 ebook.
WHEN SHMACK HAPPENS is a registered trademark of Neben Px4, LLC. TM Pending.

Cover design: Nikki Flaming/ www.flamangodesigns.com
Editing & cover text: Jenna D. Sampson/ www.jennasampson.com
Cover photo credit: Bryn Lennon

To my husband Jason.
Christ is my ROCK. Jason is my little rock.

WHEN SHMACK HAPPENS

The Making of
a Spiritual Champion

TABLE OF CONTENTS

Acknowledgments   ix

1   WHEN SHMACK HAPPENS   1
    Hard Pressed But Not Crushed

2   THE INTANGIBLES THAT MAKE A CHAMPION   7
    Laying the Foundation in God's ~~Weight~~Wait Room

3   STEPPING OUT IN FAITH   15
    When Obedience Requires Great Risk

4   LIVING AGAINST THE GRAIN   21
    Discovering God's Goals for My Life

5   DOING TIME   27
    Let the Spiritual Warfare Games Begin

6   LESSONS IN VICTORY. SEEK FIRST THE KINGDOM
    AND THEN...   33
    Winning The Tour de l'Aude

7   MELANOMA-MA-MIA   41
    A Cancer Diagnosis Just Months Before the Olympic Selection

8   EQUIPMENT FAILURE   47
     2008 Olympic Games

9   THE LITTLE RED-HEADED GIRL IS A WORLD CHAMPION   57
     Having a God Focus in a Giant World

10   FEAR   95
     The First Two Times SHMACK Happened

11   PRESSING ON AND DISCERNING THE RACE SET BEFORE US 103
     Another Crash and Another Piece of Hardware

12   GETTING DRESSED FOR BATTLE   111
     ...and Finally, Encouraging VICTORIES!

13   STANDING FIRM WHILE GOD ORCHESTRATED   119
     From 2011 World's Selection to June 2012 Olympic Selection

14   THE 2012 SUMMER OLYMPICS   129
     The Games of the XXX Olympiad

15   WHEN SHMACK HAPPENS   137
     The Post Script

EPILOGUE   143

AFTERWORD   145

ROAD RACING 101   149

CYCLING TERMINOLOGY   153

RACE WINS   156

THE DARE TO BE PROJECT   161

ACKNOWLEDGMENTS

I am where I am by the grace and hand of God. Success is always in the details, and God is the orchestrator of these details. He knew exactly what I would need and who I would need to help me along the way. Of course, it takes perseverance, patience, and perspective—but it also takes people. I know!

I have so many to acknowledge and thank. Specifically, there is my husband Jason. Christ is my ROCK. Jason is my little rock. God knew what He was doing when He paired us up. Jason's unconditional love, support, and service are beyond describable!

My parents and sister: Again their unconditional love, support, and encouragement provided me with the foundation to build on. There were also the details. My mom taught me that "cannot" doesn't exist—and spent countless hours taking me to soccer practices and games. My dad taught me to think outside the box by always finding a way to make things happen. And Brooke, who still is my best friend. I love you my hermanita! Thanks for being the best little sister ever!

My Aunt Sue, Uncle Jim, and cousins Mike and Eric: They were my second family growing up. My dad's wife Jill was another source of love toward my sister and I.

My husband's family: My *other* mom, dad, sisters, brothers, nieces and nephews. Their love, support, and prayers are treasured and needed.

I am also forever thankful for all the care, love, and time my coaches have given me. In junior high, there was Ms. Young. In high school, Coach Zimmerman was the man responsible for instilling in me the need to be a good steward of my talents. He also helped me start the process of laying down the championship intangibles. My college coach, Jay Dirksen, was there as this process continued. Then, the longest tenured, my one and only cycling coach, Dave Jordaan. He guided me from collegiate rookie to World Championships and Olympic Games. Again, success is in the details, and Dave was always behind the scenes concocting workouts and building training plans. We grew a lot together over the years. I love all of you guys!

Lana is my friend and was my angel the day I "shmacked" the wall; Christie has been there since my high school days and the "intangible" journey; Cynthia (the original muscle whisperer) and Melissa have helped me stay healthy; Kevin Rausch and Rausch PT, Hank Iglesias of Edge Cyclesports, Matt Ford and Rock N Road Cyclery, and all of my sponsors over the years; My teammates and my directors who helped me grow and always laughed (or worse) at my broccoli habits; My soingiours always doing the thankless but necessary work; Jim Safford gave me the invite to HP; Scott Warren built my first TT bike; Bob Stapleton stood by me and helped me achieve my dreams; USAC's support over the years. Thank you.

Finally, my friend in Christ, Jenna Sampson, who believed I could write a book and encouraged me along the way. Her time and ideas as an editor have also helped get the best out of me.

I haven't named everyone, but I remember you. Thank you!

CHAPTER 1

WHEN SHMACK HAPPENS

Hard Pressed But Not Crushed

Psalm 139:16
You saw me before I was born. Every day of my life was recorded in your book. Every moment was laid out before a single day had passed. (NLT)

Romans 8:28
And we know that in all things God works for the good of those who love him, who have been called according to his purpose.

Proverbs 16:9
A man's heart plans his way, but the Lord directs his steps. (NKJV)

Hebrews 12:1
"...let us run with endurance the race that is set before us,"

scan to view crash video

God knew this was going to happen. I haven't watched the video yet, but I remember it vividly. In the moment just before impact, there was an instant when I thought I had corrected my mistake, and I was going to save myself. Then, there was the next split second when I realized I was going to crash HARD. In between, I thought about how well I had been racing, and I wondered, 'Why had I done something so reckless?' Almost instantaneously, my body hurtled into the embankment, rebounded, and then collided with the ground. My face bounced off the pavement twice before I finally stopped. After this, I remember sitting on the roadside waiting for help, in both pain and in fear of what I had just done to myself, while blood poured down my nose and out of my side.

On May 17, 2013, I slammed into a rocky embankment halfway through the Amgen Tour of California Time Trial. I was racing my bike well enough to win, until I exited a technical downhill corner with too much speed. I had expected the road to straighten out—but instead there was one more chicane, and my path took me directly into the side of the mountain. Although I tried to correct my line, it was too late. My strong but small frame slammed into the rocks at over 30 mph. It was a spectacular, gnarly and horrifying crash. It was a miracle that I walked out of the trauma center with only a broken hip, ribs and nose as the video will confirm! The cameraman was actually right behind me, and the crash was seen live on NBC Universal and The Tour Tracker.

What in the wide, wide world of sports was going on? Hadn't I been through enough of these lessons—of these refining, molding and equipping events over the last decade? Hadn't I passed enough adversity tests? I was going to win that race and have a huge platform for Christ! Wasn't that the plan? My story was written, solid and powerful already. Why did this stuff keep happening?

Prior to this crash, the entire 2013 season had been a disaster. As I prepared for it, I really struggled physically. I even over-trained for the first time in my career. Then, in February, I traveled to El Salvador for my debut race with my new team—only to become dangerously ill from a local intestinal bug. March and April brought more team problems as they continued to withdraw from races on the schedule and limit my opportunities to compete. Things clearly weren't going right, and I wasn't sure anymore whether I was on the correct life path. I was in my 12th full year of competition, and I found myself asking God again if I was supposed to continue enduring this Hebrews 12:1 race of life that He (not me) had set before me. Or, was He trying to shift me out of the sport and into something different?

From January through early May, I spent time wrestling with this. As I listened for directions, God continued to open doors for me to serve Him and impact lives. In His unique way, He gave me just enough encouragement to keep PRESSING ON, while also reminding me that even though the year wasn't going well, He was working. And although my path ahead was not yet clear, it wasn't time to stop, so I continued to do what I was doing. I kept on praying for direction, I waited, and endured. However, little did I know how much I would need to endure.

That leads me into the Amgen Tour of California Time Trial on May 17. This was a huge race, and I was definitely still in the *pressing on* and *searching* mode. But the dreamer in me was also in hopeful expectation of what God was capable of doing in spite of me. In fact, the morning of the race, I prayed a Gideon-like prayer[1]: *"Lord, what do you want me doing? Can I get some kind of confirmation like you gave Gideon...just a little encouragement?? How about great legs, great mental focus and great rhythm on the bike?? Then, you do what you want with the result. If I win, I know the stage will be set for your glory."* It seemed like a reasonable request and an ideal way for God to allow me to tell the world what He had done in my life.

But often, God's ways are not our ways...and sometimes they hurt. This time I think He said, *"Amber... yes, you can share your story, but I'm giving you the opportunity to do it in a way you'd never expect, and in a way that will impact more lives than you think you can."*

So here I was confronting an extremely painful and frightening obstacle, while my season's goals were dashed and my career potentially ended. It was a

---

1. Judges 6:36-40.

huge challenge. But it wasn't the first piece of adversity—or even the second, third or seventh that I have had to face and overcome. It wasn't the first time I thought my career might be over. Yes, this was a really big hurdle, but because of these previous challenges and equipping processes, I was ready to embrace it, respond to it, and see it through God's eyes. I knew the drill.

In fact, from the ambulance to the trauma center to the acute recovery phase, I did not question God. I did not doubt God. I knew He had me. I was scared, but I was confident that His strength would be perfected in my weakness. I didn't want to be so broken and in so much pain, but never had I felt His arms hold me so tight. I just sighed and reminded God that I trusted Him, and I knew He would get me through this and do something with it. All of my previous adversities had prepared me to respond like this, and immediately, *that* peace that is beyond all human understanding began to overflow within me.

Thinking back to my prayer the morning of the crash, the interesting thing was that God actually answered my request for great legs, focus, rhythm AND a platform. I was racing with sensations that I had not had since I won the World Championship back in 2008. I was riding well enough to win. The actual physical part of the prayer was being answered. BUT. But then SHMACK happened, and my platform to share at a victory press conference was lost. Or was it?

What the devil meant for harm, God is using for His glory. He is doing something greater than I ever imagined. In my time away from cycling, He has provided me with the patience to be still, to remember all of the adversities that He has carried me through, and to write this book. He knew every step of it would be hard, so He has also given me an extra measure of peace while holding me tighter than ever as we have walked through it.

The SHMACK has put everything into motion. And once again, I am in awe as Romans 8:28 proves true while Proverbs 16:9 plays out. God is using the SHMACK both for His good and to order the steps my heart planned out. It is my hope that sharing my story of overcoming adversity will encourage more effectively than a 30-second post-race media sound bite ever could.

God's ways are certainly not mine. I know this through more ways than just this crash. Although I don't always see the good that comes out of my trials or understand the reasons why I had to face them, I choose to believe that GOD's plans are far more reaching, powerful and greater than my own. I do my best to see things from His point of view, and when it gets difficult like it did the moment of the crash, I trust Him.

My ability to respond like this was a process, though. If I had faced the SHMACK at the beginning of my career, I would have been overwhelmed or unsure of what to do. But it isn't happening then; it is happening now. *After* He has laid down a foundation of faith, perseverance, character and hope in me. *After* He has proven His faithfulness in my life over and over again. *After* He has given me previous victories to look back on. I have a perspective that comes from being molded by the master; being hard pressed but not crushed. Every time I have been asked to stand in a storm, walk through a valley, or even try to achieve something great, Christ has both provided me with His strength—and then perfected it in my weakness. It's incredible, and it has always come exactly when I needed it.

What about you? Are you ready? Jesus said, "In this world you will have trouble, but take heart, I have overcome the world." Until He returns, we will still live in a fallen world. So it is not IF, but WHEN the storms of life come. And at some point, you will face the first one or the 50th. They will come, and when they do, you will have to choose how to respond. He wrote out our days from the beginning of time. He is sovereign. He is in control. And He is with us...*always*. And if all those things are true, then we have to trust Him in the midst of these difficult episodes. (And if we are struggling to trust, then ask Him to help us!) God knows what He is doing, and He is using us for His purposes, even when they don't make sense or seem fair to us.

I have achieved 2x Olympian, 2x World Champion, and 2x National Champion status over my career, but it was far from easy. The wisdom and understanding I have gained through the process of pursuing these goals has come from watching God work in my life during this time. It has come because I have chosen to seek God, talk to Him, spend time with Him, and create that relationship that He was waiting for me to start. It has come from studying Scripture and seeing the principles of how God actively works in the lives of the people in the Bible. And lastly, it has come because I have chosen to respond to life's trials and tribulations the way I have. I have trusted God, rejoiced and given thanks. *Not* over the pain and the suffering, but in what God is doing.

My goal in writing about how I have embraced my adversity over the entire course of my athletic journey is to share a personal example of how hard the race God sets before us can be, while also demonstrating God's faithfulness, the truth of His strength and peace, and the timelessness of His word. It is also to share the source of my strength. My "toughness" is a direct reflection of Christ's power being perfected in my weakness, and this same power is available to you. Finally, I am challenging you to rejoice in your "sufferings," because they are valuable. Adversity is God's greatest tool for maturing us.

I know my stories are just centered around sports. I know you may be facing something much, much bigger in your own life (i.e. health issue, tragedy, heartache). However, the Biblical truths and attitudes necessary to respond and overcome life's storms are the same. The good news is that the strategies I have applied come from Scripture, and they can be applied to your life as well.

Come with me on a ride through the peaks and valleys of my life. But please don't see me. Instead, watch God work and recognize the process. Be encouraged! And then maybe....just maybe...you will also take away the tools to embrace adversity, to overcome it, and to become an all around champion in your own race of life.

Let's lay the foundation.

CHAPTER 2

THE INTANGIBLES
THAT MAKE A CHAMPION

Laying the Foundation in God's ~~Weight~~Wait Room

Romans 5:3-5
Not only so but we also rejoice in our sufferings, because we know that suffering produces perseverance; perseverance, character; and character, hope. And hope does not disappoint us, because God has poured his love into our hearts by the Holy Spirit, whom he has given us.

2 Corinthians 12:8-10
Three times I pleaded with the Lord to take it away from me. But he said to me, "My grace is sufficient for you, for my power is made perfect in weakness." Therefore I will boast all the more gladly about my weaknesses, so that Christ's power may rest on me. That is why, for Christ's sake, I delight in weaknesses, in insults, in hardships, in persecutions, in difficulties. For when I am weak, then I am strong.

Before I discuss how God began to lay the foundation of my own championship intangibles, I want to take you back to Egypt when the Israelites were still enslaved. Enter Moses.[1] Saved from birth, raised by the Pharaoh's daughter, educated by the best Egyptian teachers, and the man whom God chose to lead His people out of Egypt. We see God's hand on Moses' life from birth, and we are familiar with Moses' life once God spoke to him through the burning bush.[2] But if we look a little closer, there were about 40 years between Moses thinking he was ready to save the Israelites, and God actually using him. God knew Moses was not spiritually, mentally, or physically prepared to do the job ahead. God also knew he needed to give Moses the championship intangibles necessary for success. So of course, that meant God would send him out to tend his father-in-law's sheep...for roughly 40 years!

What?!

Tending sheep probably seemed like such a waste of talent and time for Moses. He probably spent years thinking about what could have been. However, if we could talk to Moses today, I bet he would admit that the prep time with Jethro's sheep prepared him perfectly for what God would ask him to do: Lead God's human sheep for 40 years while they wandered in both obedience and disobedience.

God's ways are not ours, and neither is His timing.

I was always a very gifted athlete. In fact, after I discovered my true endurance talent as a sophomore in high school, I was already planning on doing great things and winning huge races. I thought I was mature enough. I believed I was good enough. And, I even knew the verse Philippians 4:13: "I can do anything through Christ who gives me strength." I was ready to go right then and there!

However, like Moses, I was too young to know how much I still had to learn, and how unprepared I really was. But thankfully, God understood, and He sent me into His wait room for Session Number One of His molding and equipping course. He knew my faith foundation needed fortification, because the days He had written for me would require a strong faith. He knew that to

---

1. Exodus 2.
2. Exodus 3.

survive the future storms, standing very firm on The Rock[3] was going to be a necessity which meant that I needed to *know* Christ (not just *about* Him), and to know how He worked in the scriptures so that I could recognize similar tactics in my own life. And finally, in order to become an Olympian and a World Champion, I would need to develop all the non-physical tools including mental toughness, character, and perseverance. I didn't have to tend sheep for 40 years, but to start with, I would have to suffer through many injuries…and then be challenged with surrendering my own dream. But first, I had to dream.

As a freshman in high school, I was a very good soccer player, and my athletic goals were all soccer related. I wanted to earn a Division I scholarship, win a national title, and then play in the Olympics. I was serious and talented, and I believed soccer was my route. That is, until a few weeks into the school year, when I ran the mile in PE class. My PE teacher, who was also the cross country coach, recognized something very special in me, and he relentlessly recruited me to run Cross Country. He eventually convinced me that I needed to be a good steward of *all* of my talents, so I went out for his team. His persistence opened the door for my future in more ways than one!

Because of his intervention, instead of playing softball during my sophomore year, I competed in Track and Field for the first time in my life, and I ran faster than all but a handful of girls in the *entire* country in the 3200m and the 1500m. I was FAST, and I was only getting started. I quickly developed a passion to run that matched my ability, and I had a fire inside that drove me to do the little things. I wanted to work hard. I was willing to be disciplined, and I didn't have an aversion to suffering in training. As my rookie season unfolded, I recognized the special talent that my PE teacher glimpsed the year before, and I changed my focus from soccer to distance running. Right away, I locked onto new Olympic-sized goals.

But aside from that obvious door with the bright flashing lights, the other one was not apparent until I could look back at it after having walked through it. From the perspective of time, I could see that it was labeled "God's WAIT Room: Trials and Tribulations."

---

3. Genesis 49:24.

My challenges in this first "wait room" were both diagnosed and undiagnosed stress fractures. They hindered the remaining two years of my high school seasons, and then they completely derailed my collegiate hopes. In fact, the problems continued with my first step onto the campus of The University of Nebraska—Lincoln, where I had earned a full scholarship.

I had trained hard all summer and had managed to stay healthy—until the week of my departure when the pain started to return. Of course, the immature athlete in me hoped a cross-country drive from Southern California to Nebraska would provide enough rest time for me to heal, but it didn't. I tried to cover up the excruciating pain and disappointment with a limp, but instead I immediately met Nebraska's medical team who sent me in for another bone scan. It wasn't the way I had hoped to start my collegiate career, and it foreshadowed the next two years.

I faced stress fracture after stress fracture in my tibias, fibula, femurs, tibias, etc. They fractured over and over. Every time I started to come back and run well, I would get knocked back down and have to start from scratch again. And again. And again. And again. Every time, it set me back six to eight weeks away from what I loved to do. Every time, it was back to ground zero from a performance and dream perspective, while the questions and doubts rose around me.

During those four years, I became an expert cross-trainer—literally and figuratively. I read my Bible, and I talked to God a lot. I started to find nuggets in the Scripture that helped me recognize how God worked, and I continued to trust what He was telling me. Meanwhile, at the gym, I focused on what I *could* do versus what I *could not*, and I did those things for hours.

Eventually after the waiting and the rehab, I would start the agonizingly slow comeback process with the running. It was necessary, because too much too soon would re-fracture the bones. As much as I wanted to just go for a run, I had to start with only three minutes of running split up into three one-minute runs, followed by a one-minute walk. That was it. I would be done for the day. Coming back was always tedious and required tons of patience. After all, I would need to run more than 350 minutes a week to become somewhat competitive, and I was starting with only three. In addition, each of these rebuilds came after a two-month wait period, so it always took a long time to *feel* and *be* normal.

As hard as it can be to get through the 'wait,' I often think it is harder to steadfastly put in the amount of work necessary to get back to the point you were before. Doing it once is not too bad, but when you have to do it multiple times, it starts to wear on you. And over the course of the four years, I did this more times than I can remember. I would build myself up, only to get knocked back down. It was such a mental challenge to persevere and stay positive. How many times did I need to pick myself up? For a night I might think, "Enough!" But I always kept trying. I wasn't going to let go of my goals and dreams that easily.

However, eventually I had to. My body would never be able to handle what I was asking it to do. It wasn't that I didn't have the talent, the desire, or the work ethic. All of those things were overflowing within me. It wasn't my lack of trying. I had, many times. But the body that housed my gifts would not hold up, and it was my limiting factor. After two years in high school and two more years in college of struggling, I came to the realization that I needed to surrender running and the goals tied to it.

I can actually still feel the intensity of accepting that truth. I had spent the afternoon in the training room trying to get myself ready to run, but when I tried this final time, the pain was too much, and by now it was very recognizable. I knew exactly what was wrong. For some reason, I also knew that was the end. I climbed up into the bleachers at the track and I gazed out at the lanes. I was never going to achieve my dreams as a collegiate athlete, and possibly as any kind of athlete. I cried for an hour that day, and then off and on for another two years as I watched the teams compete.

I surrendered to God. I told Him that I didn't understand why he gave me such a special ability, but wouldn't let me use it. I confessed that I couldn't see the big picture, but I believed He was in control. Then, I let His grace flow over me. Over the four years of struggling, I had been learning that it was sufficient. I was grounded in Him, and I would be okay, but I was still sad because I wanted to run and compete. He had made me an athlete and a competitor! I didn't doubt Him, but I didn't get it either.

Many, many years later, I did get it. During the four years of on and off rehab—and then the next four years until I discovered cycling—I spent hours and hours riding a stationary bike developing the perfect cycling cadence and spin. I learned how to listen to my body and heed its warnings. I learned how to persevere; to keep fighting and trying. I was more mentally tough than ever. My faith had been forged in the fire. My character was molded and strengthened. Every time I was hurt, I felt God's strength being perfected in my weakness and disappointment. I had to give up the really important thing in my life (my dream), but when I did, I found out that Christ's grace really was sufficient. The championship mentality had been laid. The non-physical intangibles that I would need to survive the rest of my life were now accessible. As painful as those four years were, both emotionally and physically, I would not trade them. I would re-live them all over if I had the choice.

The main theme of that time in my life was Romans 5:3-5, and it worked because I chose to take my eyes off me and put them on Christ and His big picture. Once I did that, I could rejoice in my sufferings. Then, as I rejoiced, I learned to persevere. In persevering, I developed character in life and faith, and after the character development was started, I gained a clear picture of the hope that I have in Christ and the perspective it gives. Looking back now, I can see God's handiwork in that specific order. The courage to persevere came only after I rejoiced. The character developed *as* or *after* I persevered. The hope in Christ came as I began to understand his faithfulness and strength in response to my struggles and brokenness. In addition, the mental toughness that would be essential of me in competition, training, injury recovery, and other parts of life was being constructed and reinforced as I went through this sequence.

And possibly, the most important championship intangible that developed during this time was the creation of my life's default setting. Just as you go back to your default setting when your cell phone goes haywire, I now had a default setting to go back to when my life got intensely out of whack or presented something I didn't understand. I had felt Christ's power being made perfect in my weaknesses. I had grasped the sufficiency of His grace, and I understood what that really meant. My default setting for life was locked in. The God of the universe loved me enough to die for me, and if He loved me that much, wouldn't He want the best for me... even in the midst of a trial?

Adversity did that. More specifically, God used the adversity to prepare me physically, mentally, and spiritually for the next step. Without those four years of trials and tribulations—and then the next four years of waiting and tending the sheep specific to my own future, I would have never been a world champion or Olympian.

After all, it is not *if* you will get knocked down but *when*...and how many times? Jesus promised it. He said in John 16:33, "Here on earth you will have many trials and sorrows. But take heart, for I have overcome the world." My road ahead had all kinds of confusing, painful, and cruel times lying in wait for me. The storms were brewing, and I still needed work, but now I knew my ROCK... and the secret to overcoming.

The next question was, *Would I and could I get out of the boat and walk on water?*

CHAPTER 3

STEPPING OUT IN FAITH
When Obedience Requires Great Risk

GENESIS 12:1
The Lord had said to Abram, "Go from your country, your people and your father's household to the land I will show you."

MATTHEW 14:25-31
Shortly before dawn Jesus went out to them, walking on the lake. When the disciples saw him walking on the lake, they were terrified. "It's a ghost," they said, and cried out in fear. But Jesus immediately said to them: "Take courage! It is I. Don't be afraid." "Lord, if it's you," Peter replied, "tell me to come to you on the water." "Come," he said. Then Peter got down out of the boat, walked on the water and came toward Jesus. But when he saw the wind, he was afraid and, beginning to sink, cried out, "Lord, save me!" Immediately Jesus reached out his hand and caught him. "You of little faith," he said, "why did you doubt?"

How would you respond if God asked you to do something that required great risk? Let's assume that you hear God clearly and specifically. You know what it is He is asking you to do, but beyond that first step, you have no further direction or guarantee. You also know that from a human perspective, the risk is extreme and almost illogical. In the middle of my PhD pursuit, I began to hear God call me to do something crazy. I had to make the decision about whether to obey and get out of the boat—or to stay where I was, comfortable and safe.

After God used my distance running struggles to mold, refine, and challenge me with surrendering back to Him what He had given me, I finished out my final two years at the University of Nebraska—Lincoln. In May of 1997, I earned a B.S. in Biology. I returned to California and a month later, married my fiancé, Jason. That fall, I began graduate school at the University of California, Irvine.

I was one of a small number of individuals accepted into the Molecular Biology, Genetics and Biochemistry doctoral program. This was a prestigious program that would pay for my education and provide a monthly stipend for doing lab work[1] (which I would be doing anyway to earn the PhD). Then, assuming I eventually completed the doctorate degree, I would be in a position to get a job that could have a large salary attached to it. Furthermore, the rest of the world would think I was very smart, and my degree would be much esteemed in its eyes. It wouldn't be easy, but with effort, it was doable. It was no doubt an amazing opportunity, and I went after it the same way I chased the finish lines!

By the second year, I was ready to decide what area of research I wanted to pursue and whose lab I wanted to work in. I settled into a lab that studied Potassium and Calcium ion channels in immune cells. At first, my role as a grad student would be to take part in the research projects already operating, participate in lab meetings, keep up with my course work, and continue reading as

---

1. For the science geeks out there, I worked under Dr. Michael Cahalan in a lab that focused on ion channels in human immune cells and immune cell lines. I conducted patch clamping experiments measuring the electrical current flowing across the membranes of single cells through different kinds of Potassium channels. I also did a lot of Calcium imaging in these same cells. It was super interesting stuff, and I really enjoyed the people I was working with, but…

much as I could about my lab's field of study. In time, I would come up with my own related question to ask and answer and build a dissertation project around.

Everything was going well. My grades were good, I was actively contributing to research projects, and I was moving toward the degree. But halfway through this second year, something was changing. My head and heart were being pulled to this sport I had recently discovered.

Apparently, you could actually RACE bikes! About the same time I started graduate school, I also started mountain bike racing. Although I had surrendered my collegiate running career years earlier, the truth was that I was still an athlete and a competitor with a huge cardiovascular engine.

I was clueless about the techniques required on the dirt, though, and this lack of off road, two-wheeled experience resulted in numerous Superman-like crashes and the occasional fights with cacti and loose rocks.[2] But I was having fun, and I was not deterred. Despite these skill deficiencies, my heart and fitness still allowed me to win races and overcome my glaring weaknesses. I was always the biggest dirt magnet and the unlikeliest of victors on the podium, but I *was* on the podium. And yes, there was so much I didn't know about cycling. However, what I did know was that I still had a special, God-given endurance ability and competitive drive—and cycling was an opportunity to use them.

The reality was that I was still an athlete at heart—and not a scientist. God had made me that way when He knit my DNA together. That was always His primary plan. It was just a matter of His timing and preparation.

By early 1999, I began to see what God was doing in my heart, and how He was directing my steps. I was doing very well with the huge academic opportunity that was already in my possession, but I couldn't get my thoughts off this

---

2. I was invited out on the top secret "dirty dawn ride" by some of the best local guys around. I was a sketchy rookie, but these guys liked that I would hammer with them on the local road group rides using my mountain bike. The dirty dawn ride itself was a mountain bike ride that started before 6 a.m. and got us back in time for work (and school for me). At the end of one of these rides, I tipped over and landed in a prickly pear cactus. OUCH for both my ego and my body! The hilarious thing was that I had four worried guys pulling spines out of my backside for 30 minutes on the side of the road. Then, after riding back to campus without sitting down, I spent another two hours in the medical center while a nurse with the help of a magnifying glass pulled the remaining spines out of me. Every time I see a prickly pear, I have flashbacks!

sport that would never cure a disease or offer anything long-term in comparison to what a PhD would offer.

I couldn't let it go. Every day in the lab, instead of dreaming of a research project or being a doctor, I was dreaming of winning huge races again. My heart and gut were being tugged toward cycling. And as the tug got stronger, two things happened. I kept winning, and I discovered a coach capable of elevating me to elite status. Soon, my old dreams of becoming an Olympian were revived.

Aaaah, but this couldn't be right, could it? Why would I give up something so great to do something that didn't seem to have any redeeming value in it? There was also no assurance that I would ever make it big. My skills were not great, the salaried positions were very low and hard to find, and the Olympics were an even rarer feat. Was this a good idea? Were these my own desires? Or was this coming from God? I wasn't sure. The odds seemed close to impossible, and it just didn't seem like a reasonable option.

I did not dismiss it, though. Instead, I prayed for eight months before I spoke to anyone about it. I wanted to make sure that I was hearing God's voice and direction "to go" correctly. After all, to do it would require a great deal of courage and conviction on my side since it would be a huge risk. Once I was certain of the source of the idea, I spoke to my husband, my coach, and my academic advisor in late August 1999. Then, I initiated the move, and by December, with only a master's degree in hand, I left behind the doctoral program, the free education, and the prestigious letters that could have followed my name.

While I was praying and wrestling with God over what to do during that eight month period, I was also looking for examples in the Bible that might clue me in on God's ways for a situation like mine. For me, two of the most powerful examples were Abraham and Peter.

The first came from Genesis 12:1, where I found God's call to Abram. This was an example of God asking His child to do something risky and uncomfortable from the human perspective. God's very first instructions to Abram were to go...and then He would show him more. There were limited up-front details, but it was a definite command to do something. In my eyes, though, the crazy part wasn't that God was asking Him to do something without providing details, but what God was asking Abram to leave behind. Again, from my human perspective, looking at the short-term limited view, this just seemed wrong. But God had access to the end of the story, and as I studied Abram's call, obedience, and complete life, I could see the totality of God's plans with Abram personally—and also with the overall big picture of His redemption story. It wasn't such an unreasonable and risky request after all.

Then, there was the example with Peter, who was bold enough to get out of his safe boat and step onto the sea when Jesus commanded, "Come." Peter was a fisherman whose previous experiences had taught him that man *could not* walk on water. But when Peter took his eyes off his own limitations and placed them securely on Christ, he actually *could* do what Christ was commanding him to do. Peter got a very unique lesson in this! Of course, in that same story, he was also reminded of how easy it was to sink if his focus changed back to the storm.

I was encouraged to realize that, through Christ, nothing God would ever ask me to do would be impossible. I was also reminded how important it would be to keep my eyes fixed on Jesus. If my own focus were to change back to my limitations or the storms brewing around me, I was going to sink too.

Finally, I stumbled across Proverbs 16:9 which says, "A man's heart plans his way, but the Lord directs his steps." I began to think that maybe God had actually put these goals on my heart for His purposes. It was just that His steps ordered for me to take, were not the ones I had originally seen or tried to map out. And if that was the case, then maybe it wasn't JUST bike racing after all.

It was the combination of prayer, scripture, searching for direction, and listening that eventually got me to the point where I was ready to take the first step to leave the PhD program and chase cycling. However, it was still another year and a half before God's timing would be right for more of my path to be revealed.

This finally happened in June 2001, when I was invited to be a guest rider on a local team competing at The Hewlett Packard Women's Challenge (HP), a huge 14-day professional and international women's road cycling race. I was still a mountain bike racer, but I had failed at securing any kind of salaried position on a pro mountain bike team. And although I had not given up mountain bike racing, I had started to dabble in road cycling. This invitation to race HP would give me the chance to compete against the best in the world, albeit in a discipline (road cycling) that was not my first choice, and it would allow that Proverbs 16:9 process to come up again.

On Day 8 of that HUGE race, the impossible happened. I won! And again, God's dominoes started falling; my steps were being directed as a road racer. There had only been three other Americans who had won stages at that race, so winning a stage[3] there got me noticed by the pro team managers. In addition, the win was an automatic qualification for one of six positions on the USA World Championship team.

I was just an amateur, still learning and growing, but that win opened the door for my future. It earned me a paid position on a pro road cycling team for the remainder of the season, and qualified me for the 2001 World Championships approaching in September. Most importantly for my future, it set me up to get an offer to ride with the soon-to-be-created USA National Team, where I would stay through the 2004 season. How awesome!

The pattern I saw in Scripture, I also saw in my life. There was a call that challenged my faith and conflicted with human reason. I could hear God whispering and nudging me to do something very risky. Then, there was a response required, and I needed to take a very courageous and stupid (from the world's perspective) step of obedience before I would receive more clear directions and a better vision of the future.

And because I responded to the call, I left behind a life that would have been comfortable, predictable, and very respectable. In fact, it would have been a very good life, but because I took that risk to leave the PhD program back in 1999, and because I did not allow the pressures of the world to drown out the voice of God, I did not miss my opportunity to walk on water and experience God's best plan for my life!

---

3. A stage race vs. a one-day race: A stage race is a multiple day race. Each day of the race is labeled stage 1, stage 2, etc, and each day there is a stage winner. At the end of all the days (stages) of racing, the person with the lowest cumulative time wins the overall (also called GC) of the race and is considered the race winner. A one-day race starts and finishes on the same day, and the first person across the line is the winner.

CHAPTER 4

LIVING AGAINST THE GRAIN

Discovering God's Goals for My Life

2 CORINTHIANS 3:18

But we all, with unveiled face, beholding as in a mirror the glory of the Lord, are being transformed into the same image from glory to glory, just as by the Spirit of the Lord. (NKJV)

ROMANS 12:2

Do not conform to the pattern of this world, but be transformed by the renewing of your mind.

PHILIPPIANS 2:5-8

...have the same mindset as Christ Jesus: Who, being in very nature God, did not consider equality with God something to be used to his own advantage; rather, he made himself nothing by taking the very nature of a servant, being made in human likeness. And being found in appearance as a man, he humbled himself by becoming obedient to death—even death on a cross!

I had left the PhD behind to embark on a new chapter of my life—bike racing—because that was where God wanted me. By identifying that He made me for a definite purpose and had gifted me specifically to achieve that purpose, I could step out in faith and not look back. It may have seemed foolish or risky from the world's point of view, but from God's kingdom purpose perspective, it never was. There was no area of life that was more or less important to Him, and He needed servants everywhere, even in the world of cycling. Ephesians 2:10 said that I was God's workmanship created in Christ to do things laid out long ago for His purposes. There were hearts connected to the realm of cycling that knew of Christianity but did not know Christ. As a result, I could race bikes and serve the Lord. He would be at the core of who I was and what I was doing. And as I lived, trained, and competed in that world, my life had the potential to show people Christ. Of course, then when it was necessary, I would use words.

But in order for me to do this, I had to grasp that success starts with me seeking to be transformed into Christ's likeness. If I was going to live effectively against the grain, like Daniel in a Babylon world, then I had to reflect Christ clearly and accurately. And for God to maximize this process within the context of my own life, athletically, I had to set goals that would not impose my own limitations on His limitlessness but would instead challenge me to rely on Him. Then, as I strived to achieve them, He would be able to accomplish His own objectives in me and through me.

During the two year transition process from PhD life into full-time bike racing, God was still building on the spiritual championship intangible foundation He had already laid. However, now it was time to begin the life long process of transformation, and I needed to set my God-sized goals.

So BAM, I find myself in Lisbon, Portugal, two weeks after the September 11 terror attacks, racing the 2001 World Championships. Although there was a brief period when USA Cycling considered keeping the team home, they eventually chose to send us to compete. And before I knew it, I was in Europe for the first time.

What surreal memories I have from the entire experience! We were under constant security protection, and we had to be very careful while we travelled and then trained during the days before the race. But what an honor! I had been racing road bikes for less than a year, and now I was representing my country while competing at the highest level of women's cycling. I still remember putting on my first-ever USA jersey. I also remember wanting to win the race.

It was an intense eye opener, though. The field size was 190 riders, the racing was fast and aggressive, the roads were tiny, and I had never been in anything like it. I crashed on the first lap, but instead of drowning, I just kept fighting and surviving. At the finish, I was a long way from first place, but I was with the front group, and I believed I could succeed at this level. Something deep inside me was moved to be the best.

Five months later, in February of 2002, during my first training camp with the T-Mobile USA National Team, I laid out my short and long-term goals. I met with our team director and told him that I wanted to win the National Championships, the women's version of the Tour de France (the Tour de l'Aude), the Giro d'Italia, the World Championships, and the Olympic Games. These were the biggest races in the cycling world, and I wanted to win them. I spoke them out loud even as I rehabbed from an arthroscopic knee surgery. Why not? It was a combination of an indescribable competitive drive and a dawning realization (as scripture attested to) of how BIG my God was.

God's attributes and capacities were beyond the comprehension of my human brain and experiences.[1] If I was walking in step with Him, *nothing* would be too hard for Him to accomplish. Although my intellect saw my limitations, weaknesses, and sinfulness, my heart saw my God and His capabilities. I took myself out of the equation, and I trusted the responsibility to achieve them would be His. Then, I was courageous enough to speak them out loud and use them to pull me forward.

In May, the team flew to Europe for our first block of racing in the "big girl" world of cycling. And immediately, I achieved great results. I won my first international stage race, the Grazie Orlova Tour in the Czech Republic. Then, as the season continued, I found myself on the podium or close to it in many tough races. I placed second at the National Championships, and I was selected for the World Championships again. It was a highly successful season.

---

1. Psalm 119:1; Isaiah 40:12-12; Psalm 147:4-5.

Subsequently, 2003 picked up where the previous year left off. I trained hard but intelligently with my coach's help. I was extremely motivated, and I kept working harder and getting stronger. By the middle of the season, I had captured one of my big goals when I pulled off another 'soaring with the eagles'[2] solo victory in the USA National Championship Road Race! At this point, the trajectory of my career looked to be very promising.

It was time. About 18 years earlier (as a fifth grader), I had dreamt of making the Olympic team as a soccer player. Then 12 years earlier, I discovered my distance running talents and thought I'd win national titles and compete in multiple Olympic Games. Now here I was in my third sport, still dreaming, but finally winning the elusive first big title. These dreams that God kept writing on my heart *were* within reach. They were legitimate goals, and with my early 2003 success, I was even a favorite to make the 2004 Olympic team.

But as important to me as the cycling goals were, there was one more God-sized and God-determined goal that emerged as a result of my spiritual understanding and maturation during this time. It would be an unending lifetime process of being transformed into Christ's likeness. I would not be a useful tool for God unless He could shape me into Christ's mold. The more that could happen, the better my conduct, character, and conversation would reflect Him and the more effective my witness would be.

Even though I wasn't very far along in this process, it didn't matter. People were already watching and listening to me. In interviews or discussions, I was never afraid to credit God with my success. In addition to the verbal acknowledgements, my faith in Christ flowed out of my life naturally. People saw this, or they noticed something different about me because of it. I could see God working in their lives through it. Conversely, in my failures with these same people, I could see how important God's goal of conforming me to His likeness was. It was very possible I would be their only encounter with Christ and this goal was even more important

---

2. Isaiah 40:29-31. (In all of my early victories, the HP stage in June 2001, a stage in the 2001 Tour of Quebec, a stage in the Grazie Orlova Tour, and now Nationals, I won solo. During each of these wins, I escaped from the bunch of riders and rode alone for a considerable distance. And during each victory, this passage from Isaiah was my focal point. As I suffered and pushed on to triumph, I was soaring on the wings of eagles and not growing tired. I was riding with God! To quote Eric Liddel, "I believe God made me for a purpose, but he also made me fast, and when I run I feel His pleasure.")

than the championship cycling goals I had set. The latter would allow me to experience God's best, but the former was essential for my life to do the talking.

This confirmation process would also be an essential part of becoming a champion both spiritually and athletically. It wouldn't be easy. Being refined, shaped, and prepared rarely is. But Christ was IN me. I would make a conscious effort to submit my heart, mind, and will to Him, and I would do my best to try to imitate Him in the very non-Christian world that I was living and competing in. Then, His Spirit would do the work.

During this time, I found encouragement in Daniel.[3] God placed Daniel in a culture and world that was very opposed to what he believed, but still used Daniel's life as a witness. Even though he was in the minority, Daniel was not afraid to live out his faith. Without compromising his beliefs, he was still able to use his skills to rise from a captive to the level of a trusted advisor to the king. He held fast to his God, he lived according to God's commands, and his life reflected God without words. His actions alone spoke loudly and accurately. He was *in* the world but not *of* it.

One example came when he and the other captives were ordered to eat the non-kosher food of the King. Daniel refused to 'defile his body' by eating the royal food and drinking the royal wine. Instead, he suggested a 10-day experiment. He would only eat vegetables and drink water. Afterward, the guard could compare his appearance to the other young men. Since the official above Daniel respected him, he agreed. And 10 days later, according to Scripture, Daniel looked healthier and better-nourished than any of the other young men who ate the royal food.

A second example of Daniel's life reflecting the truth came after many years of service to the pagan King Darius. The king could see evidence of Daniel's God through his actions, attitudes, and words—and he expressed this before he was coerced into throwing Daniel into the lion's den. He hoped that Daniel's God would rescue him, and after the episode, he expected it. If Daniel's life didn't match his faith, then the king wouldn't have believed Daniel would survive the lions that night.

---

3. Daniel 1-6.

Daniel showed the introvert in me something exciting. Living for Jesus authentically would be a powerful way to intentionally and unintentionally witness and encourage on a daily basis without words. And that idea tied me back to God's primary goal for me: being conformed into Christ's likeness. If I was going to mirror Him in the midst of all my flaws, this process was crucial. Of course, then, the other secondary cycling goals fit into the territory of *who* God made me, *where* He placed me, and *how* He wanted to use me.

Daniel's life also showed me the dangers that come with living life out loud. While Daniel drew near to God, and as God blessed his efforts, challenges came in many forms because of his faith and genuineness.

In my life, I was doing my best to make God's goals *my* goals, so I would be in the best position to succeed for Him, too. As I did, the trajectory of my career was definitely moving upward, but the target on my back was also getting bigger. From a spiritual standpoint, I was becoming a threat, and after winning the National Championship, I was about to be thrown into my own lion's den.

CHAPTER 5

DOING TIME

Let the Spiritual Warfare Games Begin

ISAIAH 43:1b-3a

Do not fear, for I have redeemed you; I have summoned you by name; you are mine. When you pass through the waters, I will be with you; and when you pass through the rivers, they will not sweep over you. When you walk through the fire, you will not be burned; the flames will not set you ablaze. For I am the Lord your God...

EPHESIANS 6:10-12

Finally, be strong in the Lord and in his mighty power. Put on the full armor of God, so that you can take your stand against the devil's schemes. For our struggle is not against flesh and blood, but against the rulers, against the authorities, against the powers of this dark world and against the spiritual forces of evil in the heavenly realms.

"W*hat? I don't understand. I really do not understand. How can that be possible? It isn't possible. I KNOW it isn't possible. This is a joke, right? Right?"* I was in Italy in early July of 2003 racing the Giro d'Italia. About halfway through the 10-day race, my team director had quietly approached me after dinner to give me some bad news. I had failed a drug test.

Talk about being blind-sided. As an athlete, you try to prepare for everything. Physically, you have to be equipped for the different demands, and then mentally, you also have to be ready to endure the hard efforts while being primed to adapt on the fly when the best made plans fall apart. As much time as I spent physically preparing for races, I spent the same amount thinking through all kinds of different situations of what could go right or wrong, and what the best approach would be to meet each challenge. The scenario of testing positive had never even entered my mind as something to consider. I had never used anything illegal or questionable, nor did I ever have any intentions to do so. It wasn't who I was, and it definitely was not who Christ wanted me to be. It also would have removed my own internal driving force. I was always interested in pushing my personal limits to see how far I could go with my natural God-given abilities. If I cheated, that challenge would have been lost.

So when I heard the news, I was in total shock. My mind raced, and my heart and spirit collapsed. I had no idea how this could have happened or what to do next. I felt completely helpless, and I was scared, but I was half a world away from my husband and other support crew. Yes, I was with my team, but I could not talk to them about any of this. It was too serious, and there were too many unknowns. In addition, I didn't know if I could trust them, so I had to continue on as if nothing was wrong.

That night and for the remainder of the race, my director moved me to a single room. Now, I had the freedom to cry without questions. I also could communicate with my husband overnight. (He was in California nine hours behind the Italian time zone.) I needed his help with deciphering the USADA appeals process, finding an attorney, and tracking down the USOC ombudsman. Most importantly, though, I needed his comfort. For approximately six nights (after racing each day,) I wept with him and didn't sleep. I don't think I have ever been so tired.

The final days of that race dragged on, and I just wanted to be home. Eventually, I finished the last stage on a Sunday in Venice, and I flew back to California the next day. I was back in my own bed, but the sleepless nights continued as the battle was just beginning.

We talked to attorneys, doctors, and an athlete ombudsman. Our first step was to have the B sample tested. When it also came back positive, we knew the lab had not made a mistake with the A sample analysis. There was definitely something in my urine.[1] My only recourse would be an arbitration hearing before a three-person arbitration panel where I would be guilty unless I could prove my innocence.

While we waited for the appeal date, we did everything we could to prepare. My husband, Jason, and I spent thousands of dollars to have a specialist test my urine samples every day. We were looking for something that was naturally occurring within my body that could have caused the positive test. We found nothing. We spent thousands of dollars testing all the vitamins, herbs for colds, and green food vegetable powders that I still had in my possession—looking for some kind of contamination, but again we found nothing. I tried to retrieve the same drink mix powder, recovery protein powder, and electrolytes that the team had used during the time before I tested positive, but all of that stuff had been used up, and the containers had been thrown out long ago. We met over and over with our attorney. I researched everything I could think of, I prayed, I cried, and I prayed more. Nothing. No answers. No reasons. Only sleepless nights. Lots of them, as the battle went on for three months.

---

1. USADA and WADA are the drug testing agencies that govern Olympic sports. They are not involved with the drug testing of MLB, NFL, or NBA; only Olympic type sports. They carry out tests both in competition and out of competition. The in-competition testing happens immediately after a race. Typically, it is the race winner, race leader, and one to three random individuals. The out-of-competition testing is completely random. They can come any day at any time between 6 a.m.-11 p.m., and there is no warning. This also means they must be able to find me at any time, so I must keep my "whereabouts" on file, so they always know where I will be and when I will be there. Once I am notified of being selected for a test, I cannot go anywhere without the drug testing organization's representative. That individual must visually account for me at all times. Then, the drug testing procedure itself involves that same person, or someone additional who is female if in my case the representative is male, literally watch me pee into a collection cup. Since the bottles and all of my paperwork are identified by a number, my name is never attached to anything the lab sees and the process is completely confidential.

During this time when I should have been sleeping, I had started listening to the radio and the Bible study broadcasts that fill the overnight airwaves. I don't remember the night or the preacher, but I remember the verses from Isaiah 43: "Do not fear, for I have redeemed you; I have summoned you by name; you are mine. When you pass through the waters, I will be with you; and when you pass through the rivers, they will not sweep over you. When you walk through the fire, you will not be burned; the flames will not set you ablaze. For I am the Lord your God..." It hit me. It was not IF, but it was WHEN. I would have to go through waters and raging rivers and fires, and I would certainly feel everything. But when I did, God was not going to allow me to drown, be swept away, or burned. Instead, He would go with me through each of them. They were coming, but He would be with me. He who knew my name, would also know exactly what was happening. This passage came alive to me that night, and I wrote it on my heart. It is still one of my anchor verses.

Finally, after months of sadness and confusion, the arbitration day arrived. It was a small room with a U-shaped table. USADA (the US Anti-Doping Agency) was on one side, while my husband, attorney, and I were on the other—and the three arbitrators sat at the bottom of the U. USADA argued that their techniques and labs were sound, and that the small amount of nandrolone breakdown products they found in my sample was proof I was cheating. They assaulted me. We, in turn, defended my character. We explained what vitamins, herbs, and vegetable green food powder I had taken and why. We showed them drug test results from races nine days before—and three and four days after the positive test that were all normal. We explained that the amount of nandrolone breakdown products found in the positive test was only 1.6 billionths over the amount USADA had set as the body's natural levels, and this, in combination with the surrounding normal tests, was consistent with ingesting a tainted supplement. It would only take the amount that could stick onto the end of a pin to cause a positive, and this could easily happen in production or packaging. We even presented a peer reviewed and published scientific paper that showed 25 percent of over-the-counter supplements were tainted, and my attorney also referenced the recent case of a swimmer whose multi-vitamin had caused a positive test. It was probable that there was some level of contamination in the team's products that I was not able to test because they had already been discarded.

The circumstantial evidence was solid, and it was clear that I was not cheating. We proved my case to the arbitration panel. However, USADA's rules involved a strict liability clause. So although I had not intentionally ingested something illegal, I was still responsible. The arbitrators could only reduce my suspension from two years down to six months.

It was a victory of sorts, but it wasn't an all-out victory. I still had to do the time and serve a suspension, and I was still given a doping violation. There would be press releases, and the entire world would know the end result—that Neben was suspended because of a doping violation, while only some of that world would take time to see the entire scope of what happened to me. My integrity would be scarred, and I would always have that mark on my career. There is, and was, nothing I could do to remove it.

In addition to the public mark, I was also going to lose my best chance of making the Olympic team in 2004. At the time, I was the top-ranked ranked U.S. rider and was in great position to earn the Olympic berth. However, the suspension prevented me from racing until the spring of 2004, which effectively removed my first and best chance of making the team.[2]

As I went through this tribulation, I could easily relate to Joseph. I found myself reading and studying his story and seeing parallels within mine. God had taken Joseph on a crazy journey to get him to Egypt. Once in Egypt, God blessed Joseph greatly, and he became second to the king. His life seemed to have settled into a good place. However, Joseph got blind-sided too. He was accused of sexually assaulting Potipher's wife. Even though Joseph had done nothing of the like, and in fact had fled the situation, she was able to grab a piece of his clothing. He was innocent, but there was evidence that Joseph had been in the wife's presence, and that evidence gave him the appearance of guilt. As a result, Joseph was unfairly sentenced to prison. The charge was unfair, but

---

2. The 2004 Olympic Games selection criteria involved three ways to make the team. The first automatic selection would be the USA's #1 ranked international rider. The second would be to win a one-day time trial. The third way was to win the one-day road race. I lost my first chance because of the suspension. Then, I was second in the time trial race by EIGHT seconds. Finally, the team tactics played out in the road race, and I was not involved in fighting for a win. I would be the alternate selection for the 2004 Athens Games. This meant that I would get to fill out the forms, but I would be the first person left home.

it didn't matter. Eventually, he was released and redeemed, and God began to restore his life—with even bigger plans in his future.

I continued to trust that God would do the same with me. I also continued to pray and seek God's wisdom during my prison time. What did I need to learn? How could I grow from it? I certainly saw no good that could come out of it physically, but maybe God had something spiritual to teach me. I can't say that I know for sure if this is it, but I did begin to understand the idea of spiritual warfare and how real it was. For me, this was the first obvious time that I faced the devil's schemes (Ephesians 6:11), and realized that he was on the prowl looking for people to devour (1 Peter 5:8). If I was going to go through life drawing near to Christ and desiring to be used by Him, then I would be in a battle against "the principalities, the powers, the rulers of the darkness of this age, and against spiritual *hosts* of wickedness in the heavenly *places* (Eph. 6:12)." I would definitely need my spiritual armor (Eph. 6:10-18), I would need to encamp His mighty angels around me (Psalm 34:7), and I would need to resist the devil as James said in James 4:7.

My eyes were opened to a world that I had not wanted to admit actually existed. There was spiritual warfare going on around me. It was real, and I was knowingly facing it for the first time. However, as true as the spiritual realm of life now was to me, I was also still convinced of two things. The first was that Christ was now, and always will be, victorious in the end game, so I was already on the winning team. The second was that when this stuff came, God would be with me through the battle, and there would be greater numbers with me than with the enemy (2 Kings 6:16)!

Now, I had one more reason to pray and stand firm. I considered calling it a career at that point, but I did not give up. That was not God's plan. I needed to stand firm, and then I needed to press on! Little did I know, that God had bigger plans for me up ahead.

CHAPTER 6

LESSONS IN VICTORY. SEEK FIRST THE KINGDOM AND THEN…

Winning The Tour de l'Aude

Matthew 6:33
But seek first his kingdom and his righteousness, and all these things will be given to you as well.

Psalm 55:22
Cast your cares on the Lord and he will sustain you; he will never let the righteous be shaken.

Psalm 37:4
Delight yourself also in the Lord, and He shall give you the desires of your heart. (NKJV)

The drug suspension had been reduced by the arbitration panel to the minimum under the letter of the USADA law. However, I still had to serve six months, and it was not removed from my record. So from the moment the press release went around the world, I wanted to make everyone see what had happened and how unfair it was. I wanted them to believe in me, and what I stood for. I was honest, and my God was real, and it hurt that I couldn't erase the damage completely. Eventually, I accepted there would always be doubters, and I pushed forward knowing the truth of the matter and that God was still in control; even of this. I stopped focusing on what could have been, and instead looked at what was still in front of me. The reality was that I still had a chance to make the 2004 Olympic Team through the automatic spot given to the winner of the Trials race, and I also still had many goals after that. It was time to continue on my journey in sport and with the Lord. There were huge victories to come, but one small challenge first.

It was an eight second test, courtesy of the Olympic Trials. Even though I rode very well in the event, eight seconds separated me from my dream. I finished in second place and was the first one left home. One alligator, two alligator, three alligator...EIGHT! I was eight seconds from an Olympic berth.[1] So close...yet... so far. I would have to wait another four years until I'd have another chance.

In that moment of defeat, everything came hurtling back at me. I agonized over the race, my efforts, and the temperature and wind changes between my start time and the one person who beat me. I felt so wronged again by the tainted supplement and the suspension, and I felt like the 2008 Olympics seemed so far away with no guarantees that I would be good enough or healthy enough to try to qualify again. I didn't want God to say *wait* once more, or to find a new way to ask me if I trusted Him, but He did.

He knew I wasn't ready, and the timing still wasn't right from His standpoint, so it was necessary for me to respond accordingly. I reminded myself of

---

1. To this day, my coach will not let me forget. As I get close to a big race he will find a way to work "8 seconds" into the conversation. Honestly, it's not a very good motivational tactic, but I understand his point. It is a reminder to give more than 100% from the start line until I cross the finish line, so there are not ever any *coulda-woulda-shouldas.* I might win or lose by less than a second or by 8, but if I have done my best, there are no complaints.

His awesomeness and power, and I returned to my default setting of knowing this same God loved me enough to stretch out His arms on a cross and die for me. His power was infinite and His love perfect. I could trust His methods and the step-by-step route I was walking on, but the human in me still continued to wrestle with the idea of making God's goals mine, while fitting my riding objectives into my role within His big picture Kingdom plans.

My immediate answer was to keep doing what God made me to do so that He could continue His work *in* me and *through* me. He had me where He wanted me. I couldn't see it, but He could, and my responsibility at that time was to be a good steward of my cycling talents.

The most effective way to do this would be to race full time against the best in Europe. There, I could improve my tactical skill and fitness levels. However, at the end of 2004, to date there had only been one or two other American women cyclists to ride for a European-based team, and no one was currently doing it. I would be entering unfamiliar territory. Nevertheless, I was very serious about achieving my ultimate race objectives, and since my current team would only be competing in America during the upcoming season, the decision was easy. I left a comfortable situation with T-Mobile-USA and signed a contract with a new Dutch team, Buitenpoort-Flexpoint.[2]

It turned out to be a remarkable fit. I was the only American on a team with women from the Netherlands, Denmark, Germany, the Czech Republic, Sweden, and Switzerland. I was immersed in an environment that was real and professional. We worked hard together, we trusted each other, and we won a lot of races. We were a low-budget (but super pro) team taking on the big powerhouses...and winning!

I was living the cycling dream, and I was also doing my best to be a servant. My team was filled with very talented and accomplished riders, and I wanted to

---

2. During my four years with Team Buitenpoort-Flexpoint (or just Flexpoint), my salary was only 1000E/month (or $1,340). I removed money from the equation when I made the decision. I raced almost exclusively in Europe. I would start the season with the Redlands Classic in California in March, and then I would move to Europe for 2-2.5 months to live and race. After that big chunk, I would fly back and forth for 3-4 week blocks of time throughout the remainder of the season. When I was in Europe, I was focused on racing. When I was home, I was focused on training. The reason for doing that was so I could see my husband. He had a real job and his teaching schedule didn't allow for travel time!

help them while I developed as an athlete. Even though I had my own race targets, our team goals were most important, and this situation actually presented me with the perfect challenge to imitate Jesus. Specifically, I wanted to try to lead by serving, just like Jesus did when he washed the disciples' feet.

In May of 2005(still my first year with Team Flexpoint), we competed in The Tour de l'Aude, the hardest race on the women's calendar—and at the time, considered the women's version of the Tour de France. Even though we were an underdog team, I believed we had a great chance to win. I was riding very well, and I was excited and motivated to work hard for my teammates. I was also prepared to do my part with a "service first" heart and mindset, both on and off the bike.

Surprisingly, on the fourth day of racing and serving, an opportunity knocked on my door, and I didn't hesitate to answer it. There was a break of four riders up the road and a need for someone on my team to get to it. Instinctively, I reacted and jumped across. Nobody else in the peloton responded behind me, and I rode from the group to this break alone. Shortly after I arrived, we came to a climb, and I attacked the other girls, leaving them behind and riding solo to victory on top of the hill. It was a HUGE win! The biggest of my career to date! And on top of the stage win, I was now leading the overall classification of the race, meaning that I had earned my first yellow jersey.

I continued to race with an intelligence and strength that I'd never had. My hard work was paying off, I was reading the races correctly, and my body was responding to the years of disciplined training. During this time, I was constantly talking to God and reading through the Psalms. I was still trying to seek him first and to serve. It was awesome stuff. I could feel His presence with me, and I felt like I was finally on the same page with Him.

I still had one stage left, though. It was the "queen" stage, involving a long 25km HC(hors categorie) climb, a super technical descent on a narrow, twisty, old road, followed by a little reprieve, and then a final 7km climb to a ski station. It was the hardest of the 10 days of racing, but it fit my strengths, and I just had to keep doing what I'd been doing. I had more than a minute lead, and I was in an excellent position to win a GRAND TOUR!

At the top of the HC climb I was feeling great, and I was only with one other rider. However, this rider was the best descender in the women's peloton, and she managed to put more than a minute on me over the course of the treacherous, wet, and cold downhill. This was enough time to make her the virtual leader on the road, and it left me with a large deficit to make up!

I started to scrap and ride hard on my own. I had to mentally recover quickly and then respond immediately. Slowly, I reeled in and then dropped all but the one rider who had caught and passed me on the descent. She was still far enough ahead to win the race unless I could make up a one minute, 30 second deficit.

I fought with every ounce of strength I had. I started the final 7km climb closing the gap to the overall victory, but I was still about a minute behind. I was suffering badly as I pushed beyond my physical limits. Every muscle in my body was burning, and I was exerting so much effort, my tongue was tingling, and the pressure in my head made my eyeballs feel like they were going to pop out. Mentally, I was blocking out all of those feelings and willing my body to keep going. My team director was on the radio encouraging me and pushing me to do the same. He wanted this just as badly as I did!

In the midst of this zone of effort, focus and pain, my Bible passage from the morning came back to me. It was the verse from Psalm where God tells me if I give Him my burden, He would not allow me to be shaken. In a left-hand switchback corner on the climb, I specifically remember thinking...God you promised that I would not be shaken, and He seemed to say back to me, "You won't. Trust me and fight to the very end." So I did.[3]

But with 1km to go, I was still four seconds behind. My director started screaming over the radio at me "Four f***ing seconds. Come on. Four f***ing seconds!!!" I kept digging. I thought I was going to fall off my bike, but I just kept digging all the way across the line. I knew God had me.

I crossed the finish line frozen and exhausted. I wanted to collapse right there, but I managed to ride over to the team bus where I would wait for the results. Finally, they came. WOW. I had just won this HUGE, 10-day stage race by 1/10 of a second. Impossible, right? I smiled on the inside. God had not allowed me to be shaken, and He blessed me with a great victory. It was a small reward, but a huge piece of encouragement for me. God challenged me on that

---

3. The idea is that God's word speaks to us exactly where we are. It is timeless and applicable. We just need to be in it, so He can speak; and be sensitive to it, so we hear. Nothing is too small or big for God to care about.

final ascent, I believed Him, and He didn't allow me to be shaken.

I left that race with the sensation that I was walking in step with Christ as I moved forward with my life and the immense cycling goals that were a part of it. It was clear that I could serve God's purposes directly or indirectly right where I was as a bike racer by doing the simplest of things. The secret was making Christ my priority. If I could, everything else would fall into place just as Jesus had said in Matthew 6:33: *But seek first his kingdom and his righteousness, and all these things will be given to you as well.*

Similarly, the commands of Psalm 37 included one to delight in the Lord. By delighting in the Lord, God's desires would become mine, and I would be on track. This hit home for me, and I understood how essential it was to make time for Him; to bring Him into each aspect of my life; and to enjoy conversing with Him. He definitely belonged above everything, but during this time, I also grew to *want* to put Him above all and to have our goals match. In the midst of my years with Team Flexpoint, I started to practice these principles.

I had huge dreams in sport and a longing to be used by Him through it, but the overriding prerequisite was getting my life priority right. It was

CYCLING SPEAK

Professional Team Racing: Each team has 12 riders on the roster but only 6 in the race. The team consists of riders who are climbers, sprinters, time trailers, workers (domestiques), and all arounders. The idea is that, together as a unit, the team can help the rider whose specialty best fits the terrain and nature of the race. The racing season begins in March and ends at the World Championships in September.

Yellow Jersey: During the race, the race leader has the honor of wearing a yellow jersey. The leader often changes each stage. Whoever is wearing it after the final stage is the winner of the race!

Peloton: The main pack of riders during a race.

obvious, but not always easy because of the many distractions of the day to day world combined with the tug of earthly achievements and adulation. But when I was walking with God and in that "spiritual zone," my life really was ordered properly. God wasn't just a single piece of my life's pie; He was the central focus of every portion of it. My greatest challenge would be to make this a daily point of emphasis as I kept succeeding on the bike.

And the success continued the entire period of time with Flexpoint. In May of 2006, I went back to the Tour de l'Aude as the defending champion.[4] Of course, I faced more challenges, but I won it again! A feat that no other American and very few Europeans had ever accomplished. Then, in 2007, I was in a position to go for three wins in a row, but I sacrificed my own victory to help my teammate preserve hers. In addition to my triumphs in France, there

Race Stages: Each road race has multiple stages. Basically, the race is broken down into many mini-races—one each day. The first to reach the finish line each day has won that stage. The overall leader of the race wears the yellow jersey and is the rider with the fastest time (cumulative) over all the stages to date. There can be up to 10 stages in a road race. In my first two years (2002 and 2003) there were two races that were 14-day races. After the 2003 season, these races disappeared from the calendar and the longest today are 10 days.

were numerous other high-level international races where I was either winning or finishing on the podium, including multiple 2nd places in the two other Grand Tours on the women's calendar—The Giro d'Italia and Thueringen Rhundfart.

Since the 2004 Olympic Trials, I had established myself as one of the best stage racers in the world, and one of the top racers in America. In fact, I was once

---

4. After I won the Tour de l'Aude the first time, I became the poster girl for the race for the next three years. My mug was plastered all over the city of Carcassone and the l'Aude region. There it was on bus stops and big billboards. It was also on the cover of the race book, but it was the most fun to see the giant versions of it all over town.

again the highest-ranked rider from the USA after the 2007 season. With 2008 FINALLY on the horizon, I was primed to make a run at the Olympic team and take a shot at gold!

If only it were so easy, though. God is the ultimate teacher and equipper, and the author of our life stories. And just as my muscles and body required the constant stresses to continue to adapt, improve, and become even more useful, my spiritual muscles needed the same. It was time for another round of strengthening, refining, and preparation courtesy of the six-letter "C" word. Cancer.

CHAPTER 7

MELANOMA-MA-MIA

A Cancer Diagnosis Just Months Before the Olympic Selection

1 Thessalonians 5:18
give thanks in all circumstances; for this is God's will for you in Christ Jesus.

2 Corinthians 1:5
For as the sufferings of Christ abound in us, so our consolation also abounds through Christ. (NKJV)

1 Chronicles 28:9b
...for the Lord searches all hearts and understands all the intent of the thoughts. (NKJV)

It was sometime in August 2007 when my husband asked me what was on my back. I hadn't even noticed the small, dark-colored, flat mole until that question. The initial inspection didn't cause alarm. I thought it looked a little questionable, but I didn't think anything further of it. However, over the course of the next six weeks, I kept re-examining it, and the more I looked at it, the more I thought it didn't seem normal. The border was irregular, the color was weird, and it was changing. [1]

Finally, in late September while I was in Stuttgart, Germany, racing in my sixth World Championship,[2] I contacted a pediatrician friend to ask for a skin doctor referral. By that time, I was getting a little nervous, and I wanted to get the mole checked out as soon as I could. My season would be over after this race, and the offseason that started in October would be a good time for me to take care of it.

I was not expecting the worst, but the doctor's reaction told me something was amiss. Although there was a calmness to her, there was also an urgency and a seriousness in her response. She explained that the normal procedure was to scoop off a questionable mole and have the tissue sent to pathology for analysis. But in this case, she believed the mole required a more intrusive action. She wanted to cut out a larger section of tissue that would require stitches and leave a one-inch scar behind. That would allow her to get underneath it completely and have a more comprehensive section of tissue available for testing. I agreed to it, and minutes later, she was giving me a lidocaine shot and slicing me up with her scalpel. After, she cauterized it, sewed it up, and told me I would receive the results in three days.

But less than 24 hours later, my phone rang. It was my dermatologist personally calling with my test results. I knew this wasn't normal procedure. It was too fast, and it was actually my doctor calling—not the office. My insides started to melt as I listened to her explain that she had good news and bad news. The good news was that she thought we got it early, and she was very thankful

---

1. The ABCD's of skin care: Asymmetry, Border irregularity, Color, and Diameter. Regular skin checks are so easy! Don't be afraid to get them.

2. It was the 7th time I had been selected to worlds, and the 6th time I was competing. The year of my suspension, I could not compete.

she had taken out the larger section of tissue. The bad news was that the mole was a melanoma, a very serious and aggressive form of cancer. I would need to see a specialist to have further blood work done, get his opinion on the tissue analysis, and make a plan for moving forward.

Whoa. I had cancer. I guess I thought it might be cancerous; otherwise I wouldn't have taken the initiative to schedule an appointment. However, I honestly did not expect it to be that bad. I was too young and healthy, and I was on a mission to make the Olympic team. I didn't have time for cancer, nor did I want it. But right then, I had it. And as soon as I received the news, my mind began to race in every direction.

What was God doing? How would I tell my family? What would the treatment be like, and how long would it take? If we could treat it, how fast could I get back to training? Would I die? I knew that was an option and that God may have a purpose with it, but I was still reluctant to accept it. I did not want to leave my husband alone, nor did I want my family to have to deal with losing me. Maybe God would work a miracle and remove the cancer? That was always possible.

I was numb. Cancer is a powerful word, and to be directly associated with it was very surreal. However, I was not entirely surprised in the sense that my journey as an athlete had already taken me over some interesting obstacles, which I did not always understand. Through each of them, though, God had brought something positive, and I believed this would be no different. This was just a new story, or a new chapter, that He needed to write into my life. My faith reaction was simply to say, "Ok Lord...what are you going to do with this? What do I need to learn?" And I also asked, "Does it have to be a long chapter?"

Then, I gave thanks. God commands us to give thanks IN ALL circumstances, so I chose to try. I thanked Him for His grace and love and for holding me in His arms in the moment. I knew He would also continue to do the same as we walked through it. I also actually thanked Him for it, because I believed He would use it to do something special in a life that I may or may not ever know.

In giving thanks, my perspective and focus was immediately shifted back to God and His power, purpose and eternal plans. Anything I faced right then would be limited compared to the infiniteness of eternity. In addition, I always had access to Christ's power and peace and *this* was another opportunity for me to take it. I just had to keep looking at Jesus and not the cancer.

For two weeks I was challenged to focus on Him while I anticipated what my melanoma doctor would tell me. I wanted to know right away what I was dealing with, and what the endgame results would be, but I had to wait. And as I waited, I had to trust. And as soon as I drifted away from trust and got caught up in dwelling on the possible outcomes, I would have to consciously bring my focus back to Christ.

Eventually, the important appointment came. I met with Dr. James Jakowatz, a surgical oncologist and the director of the Melanoma Center at the UC Irvine Medical Center. He explained the pathology report and agreed that it was only a stage 1 melanoma. However, he would not be sure if it had spread to the lymph nodes or elsewhere until further testing was completed. He would need to surgically remove a greater perimeter of tissue around the original source. I left this meeting with a great deal of hope, but still a little bit of apprehension.

The next week, I emerged from surgery with a new 11cm scar that paralleled my spine on my mid-back. The cut was very deep and extremely painful. The pain surprised me, but in the end it was all worth it. The further tests and tissue pathology showed that the cancer was contained to the back, and it had not spread. The doctor was happy and believed he had cut all of it out. As a result, I would not need any further treatment, but I would have to monitor it closely for the next five years, and then see my oncologist regularly for the rest of my life.

If cancer could be easy, mine was. I was blessed to have caught this in a very early stage where the cure rate was 99%. I was also blessed to have great doctors recognizing and responding accordingly, and of course, to have God's gracious hand on me.

My post-surgical recovery was fast. For the first 48 hours, I had to be extremely careful not to pull the tissue apart or to allow the wound to get infected. This limited my activity, but only for the first two days. After my sports doctor told me that sweat would not cause infection, nor would I pull the skin apart by riding if I stayed "tranquilo,"[3] I rode my bike on my trainer for the next 12 days until my follow up appointment with my surgical oncologist. Then, two weeks after surgery, "Dr. Jak" gave me the green light to go outside with the best prescription ever: "Go live your life, Dude!"

So I did! I met with my coach, Dave Jordaan, and we created a training plan for the winter—and a game plan for making the 2008 Olympic Team. I also committed to a biannual date with my oncologist—and an additional two checkups with my skin doctor for the next five years. I was back in business!

In the haze of facing another challenge, I found comfort in the apostle Paul who faced more adversity than I did! Paul was put into prison often, whipped too many times to count, and faced death over and over. He was tortured, beaten, shipwrecked, and adrift at sea. He faced dangers from robbers, rivers, the Jews, the Gentiles, and false believers. He faced dangers in the cities, deserts, and the seas. He went without food, drink or sufficient clothing to stay warm.[4] But in spite of all of those obstacles, Paul continued to endure in order to serve Christ! How was that possible?

Paul had two perspectives that kept him pressing on. His life had been transformed by an encounter with Christ that submerged him into the depths of God's unconditional love. He was a man on the complete opposite end of the spectrum with regards to God—a murderer and the self-labeled chief of sinners—until that meeting where Christ made him new and changed his life. Second, Paul was given a glimpse of heaven that allowed him to recognize that his eternal glory would easily outweigh any amount of momentary suffering that he would face on earth.[5] The combination of those two truths in Paul's life gave him the vision to see beyond his hardships—and empowered him to press on.

Then, in the midst of all of his struggles, I think Paul always saw God working, either in him or in others. Christ's power was constantly being made

---

3. After spending much of my racing career in foreign countries, I've enjoyed picking up other languages and adding them to my vocabulary. As you may have guessed, this is Spanish or Italian for calm or relaxed.

4. 2 Corinthians 11:23-27.

5. 2 Corinthians 12:1-4; 4:17.

perfect in his weakness. Everywhere he went, he witnessed by word and action. And as a result of facing so much adversity, he was uniquely equipped to be able to encourage and comfort others.[6] Paul knew God had a purpose for him, and the hardships were a part of that process. I started to see the same in my own life.

My encounter with the six-letter "C" word also brought about a "motive check" for me. After three years of success, did my goals still match God's goals for my life? Did I still want success His way? What was the condition of my heart, and where were my motives?

God weighs and searches our hearts, and He understands our intentions.[7] I used this time to take a hard, honest look at myself. Was I, like Paul, more worried about the future glory, or had I gotten too focused on the earthly rewards (the wood, hay and stubble)? It was good for me to think about. Pride is subtle but dangerous, and doing a motive check on my heart was a good idea at this time.

As I entered into the winter of 2007, after beating cancer, I started to train again for the 2008 season. I finally felt like I was fully equipped and ready. I had faced the fires of life through athletics—and now a brush with cancer. I felt like my heart was in the right place, and my focus was on Christ and making Him known. I was delighting in Him and trusting Him, and my experiences had refined and built my faith and character. I knew that when I was weak, I was actually strong, because *less of me* meant *more of Christ*. I could speak from a place of experience just as Paul could. God's power, greatness and limitless abilities were real to me. I knew I could do anything He asked me to do. I believed it! AND I wanted to do it! I was waiting…

---

6. 2 Corinthians 1:3-7.

7. Proverbs 21:2; 1 Chronicles 28:9.

CHAPTER 8

EQUIPMENT FAILURE

2008 Olympic Games

Proverbs 16:9
A man's heart plans his way, but the Lord directs his steps. (NKJV)

Proverbs 3:5-6
Trust in the Lord with all your heart, and lean not on your own understanding; In all your ways acknowledge Him, and He shall direct your paths. (NKJV)

A fter fully recovering from the cancer scare, I thought the obvious way to glorify God would be by winning an Olympic gold medal. It would be a powerful platform for God to show his awesomeness through the story of my life, and it fit with the dream that had been on my heart since I was a fifth grader.

Of course, before I could win, I needed to make the team, and being good enough to make it was dependent on my off-season training. Thankfully, by the grace of God, the training from late November 2007 through March 2008 had gone exactly as my coach and I planned. November and December had been filled with endurance base riding and on-the-bike strength work; and then January through March brought in the long intervals of steady state threshold work that was my bread and butter. Once the middle of March came around, it was time to start the early season racing which I would use to get the very short, hard efforts necessary to raise my 'top end'[1] fitness. Through the entire offseason, I was able to stay injury-free and complete all of the prescribed training.

Consequently, as the 2008 season progressed through June, I was riding better than ever. I didn't win anything, but I hadn't been concerned with achieving personal results in these early races. I was prepping to be at peak form in August in anticipation of making the Olympic team. And by doing a lot of work for my teammates, I was playing a role that allowed me to do my job while pushing my own limits without the fear of failure. As a result, I was getting stronger and fitter with each passing month. It was the perfect plan, because if I was to be selected, I wanted to be ready to medal.

Finally, in late June, the selection decision was announced. Four years after the "eight-second heartbreak," I received the phone call from USA Cycling telling me that I had made the team! Whoohoo! I was a USA Olympian—one of three people selected in the discipline of Road Cycling.

---

1. Think of a pyramid. The widest portion at the bottom, and the first part to be built is the aerobic base. I am required to put in a lot of time at this effort level, but physically I can. It is not too debilitating. Once the base is built, I can ride harder. As the intensity level goes up, the total amount of time spent in it gets smaller. The very top of the pyramid, which is built last, represents the maximum level efforts. Only a short amount of time relative to the total training time can be spent here. They are very hard intervals and require more recovery, but are an essential part of training after the previous portions of the pyramid have been built.

What a huge honor! There were only 596 total athletes sent by the US Olympic Committee; 286 women and only 3 for my sport. It was not an easy thing to do, and in fact for me, it had been a lifetime in the making. To make the team was beyond words.

The Olympic Games transcends sport. Very few people may know or understand what road cycling is, but everyone knows what it means to be an Olympian. It's the one thing you can do that lifts you to a level that people appreciate. I hadn't just been riding my bike all the time. I had been training, working, preparing, and trying to reach the pinnacle of sport, and now, I didn't look so crazy!

The Olympic Games experience was something I will never forget, and it started before we left the U.S. with "processing" in San Francisco. Olympic processing was where every U.S. athlete stopped before departing for Beijing—to fill out all of the necessary paperwork, get a medical check, take some official photos, go through a few mandatory meetings, and most importantly, pick up ALL of the U.S. Team gear!

We actually took a shopping cart through a warehouse of clothing and shoe stations to pick up piece after piece of the Nike and Ralph Lauren clothing assigned to the athletes. We would be required to wear this stuff 100 percent of the time while we were in the village and at the Games, so it was very important. It was also very fun. When it was over, I had two huge suitcases full of clothing.

From processing, I traveled directly to Beijing with many other USA team members. And as soon as we stepped off the plane, I knew this was going to be different. There were already media members from all over the world stacked up to capture the arrival. It was just the start of the hoopla that comes with the Olympic Games.

Before I could go anywhere or do anything, though, I needed to pick up my official credential. This was gold. It was my ticket everywhere, and it identified me as an athlete. Except when I was racing, I wore it everywhere.

Once I had my credential, I could access everything I needed as an Olympian, including the Olympic Village. The village was a large, secured area that became a small western city within the eastern world of China, and it was where all of the athletes and coaches resided during the Games. Walking into it for the first time was very overwhelming. The aura of the Olympics and the presence of greatness filled the air, and the anticipation and excitement were almost maxed. Everywhere I looked, there were athletes from every country and discipline. I immediately sensed a level of respect being shared between everyone. Any athlete who had made their own team knew exactly what it took to get there. There was a mutual respect regardless of sport. As the entirety of it all soaked in, I realized that I was one of those athletes—and that I belonged. It was very humbling.

Within the village, the cafeteria was the one place where every athlete went. It was the ultimate food court, spreading out for what seemed like forever, offering food from every corner of the world, and staying open 24 hours a day. It was also immense enough to hold rows and rows of tables and chairs for dining, hanging out, and people watching. (In fact, it was one of the best places ever for people watching because any body type or skin color could be found!)

As excited as I was to compete, first came the Opening Ceremonies and a decision. Since the road cycling race for the women was the second day, I wasn't sure if I should participate in the long, ceremonial walk around the stadium. However, I had already planned my training in a way that allowed me to accommodate for the extra stress, and I knew there was an "early exit" option for the athletes who wanted to march through the stadium and leave immediately without having to stand around for the event to finish. After thinking long and hard about it, I decided it was possible to walk without it impacting my preparation for the race. It turned out to be a great decision.

The day of the opening ceremonies was awesome! Late in the afternoon, I met up with the U.S. contingent of athletes and staff. It was too early to stage with the other nations for the ceremonies, but we had one surprise meeting to make first. We were bused to a secure arena for an in-person pep talk by President Bush, our official team leader! As we all listened intently, we were just Americans, not Republicans, Democrats, or Independents—just Americans united as Team USA. It was a special moment, and we were pumped.

After the speech, the president went around to each team to shake each athlete's hand and take a team photo. He eventually made it around to the cycling group. As he shook my hand, I told him he should try road cycling sometime, and that I would be happy to take him out for an easy ride. He smiled and looked me in the eye. Then, as we were setting up for the group photo, he actually turned back and looked at me again. He grabbed my hand and asked me to stand next to him. It was priceless. The active President of the United States of America had his arm around me while we smiled for our group shot. It was possibly my favorite memory from the Games.

After the meeting with the President, all of the U.S. athletes moved to the official staging arena where all of the nations waited until their name was called. The United States of America was one of the last names to flash on the arena screen, but once it did, we lined up outside to enter into The Bird's Nest, the stadium where the ceremonies were taking place. As we walked under the stadium as one unit, the excitement was building and a spontaneous chant of "U-S-A! U-S-A!" broke out. I had chills. I had to fight back the tears, as right at that moment, it really hit me. I *was* an Olympian.

As we came out from under the stadium and entered onto the track, the lights were extremely bright, and the flash bulbs flashed non-stop. The flags, the colors, and all the people...it was incredible. The noise was deafening, yet at the same time, it wasn't. For me, it was similar to one of the rare moments in competition when you go into "the bubble," a zone where you are aware of everything and are taking in every detail, but your world becomes quiet. I was so glad I had chosen to attend.

Two days later, it was our event day, our moment in time, and I felt mentally and physically ready. I had prepared years for this one day, and it was finally time to show the world what I was made of...on an Olympic stage. I was excited, and I had all my butterflies moving in formation!

Before the race started, I did some warming up in the limited area we had access to. It was oppressively hot in Beijing, so I didn't want to do too much. However, I did want to make sure that my equipment was working properly. The last thing I wanted was for my bike to fail when the rest of me was in peak form. I checked, double-checked, triple, and quadruple-checked my bike and shifting. The gears were good, and I couldn't make the chain fall off, even with a very intentional effort to do so. I was using a compact crank, so I wanted to protect myself from that very scenario. Dropping a chain is rare, but the potential is greater with a compact crank, so in checking my bike, I deliberately did everything wrong with my shifting to try to make this happen. When I could not, I returned to our pre-race tent, satisfied that my equipment was working perfectly.

Finally, the race started, and we rolled very slowly out of Tiananmen Square and down the main streets of Beijing. The first hour of the race was very easy. The air was very polluted, the heat index was off the charts, and the race would be hard in the final hour and a half when we entered the Great Wall climbing circuits—so everyone was reluctant to start riding too hard, too early. I didn't mind, because it gave me a chance to relax and soak in the grandiosity of the race.

Surprisingly, about one hour into the race, the weather changed dramatically, and the skies opened up with massive waterfalls of rain. The water started to fill the roads. Literally, we rode our bikes through standing water that was 6-12 inches deep in some areas. It was crazy. Then, as we got closer to the Great Wall, the racing difficulty increased, and the intensity, combined with multiple crashes, quickly made things chaotic.

As we came up the road that would take us onto the Great Wall circuit, the rain was still pouring down, and the temperature was still dropping. I was in my own special zone, focused and staying toward the front of the bunch where there was less danger and chaos. But for some reason, my eye caught a huge American flag. I glanced left and saw my husband, my sister and her husband, and my youngest sister-in-law holding this flag and screaming my name at the top of their lungs! It was just enough of a glimpse to lock down that memory forever.

Shortly after seeing them, we rode straight onto the Great Wall circuit. We would ride it twice before the finish. Each lap would take us up a long climb and bring us back down, before a final kick up to the finish line. Entering the circuit, I remained relaxed, alert, and aware of the race tactics playing out. I was still in good position relative to the entire field of riders, and I was patiently saving my energy for the next lap. My years of experience had taught me that the winning move in a championship event would not happen until then.

When we started the climb on the final lap, I was positioned perfectly within the first handful of riders sensing the race-changing attack was about to come. I knew I had the ability to go with it, and once I did, I would be in a position to win a medal. As I anticipated this move, and while the chain was in the middle part of the rear cog set, I shifted to the small ring. But when I did this, something I had done thousands of times before, my chain fell off and jammed between the crank and the bike frame. When I tried to pedal the chain back on, which is normally possible, it did not work. I started to drift backwards through the peloton as I tried over and over again. But as I was doing this, the attack came, and the race went up the road. I couldn't even try to follow. Instead, I had to stop, get off my bike, and un-jam the chain.

There were 23 years between me dreaming of being an Olympian and actually being in the Olympics, and then—just 10 kilometers from the finish line—my equipment failed. It was not my head, my legs, my lungs, or my heart. It was the stupid drive train, and it failed in a way that I had quadruple-checked beforehand. I stood there on the side of the road, pulling on my chain, while I could see the girls riding up the road, the motorcycles with the cameras speeding by me, and my hopes being washed away. It was a moment of extreme emotional pain. It would have been different if my body had failed; but it wasn't that I had tried and failed. Instead, I never had the opportunity to try, and it hurt unlike anything I had ever experienced.

I refused to quit, though. I got back on my bike and pedaled up the road. I caught group after group, but I couldn't make it back to the front. I crossed the finish line in a disappointing 33rd place—drenched, frozen, and mentally, physically, and emotionally exhausted. This was not what I had expected to happen at my first—and possibly only—Olympics, and I couldn't get a do-over. The tears poured out that night.

In my heart, I cried out to the LORD just like David had done so many times through his own journey. I wanted to be mad at Him, but I couldn't for long. I had too many other life experiences and challenges where He had made His faithfulness and comfort in my brokenness real. I had too much knowledge of who God was, and what He had already done. And I knew, right then, He was still working for His own purposes. Although I preferred a different ending to my Olympics, I reminded myself of Job's response when he said, "I know that you can do all things; no purpose of yours can be thwarted. You asked, 'Who is this that obscures my plans without knowledge?' Surely I spoke of things I did not understand, things too wonderful for me to know."[2]

I was also reminded that I am a jar of clay molded by the Master. In fact, all the years of being shaped and refined filled me to the brim with a strength, peace and hope that could only come from Christ. And now, as a result of my equipment failure, I had a new crack created on the world stage giving that treasure a chance to flow out. In fact, Paul described it like this: "...we have this treasure in jars of clay to show that this all-surpassing power is from God and not from us. We are hard pressed on every side, but not crushed; perplexed, but not in despair."[3] Through the lifetime process of persevering in preparation of the Olympic Games, I had gained this treasure; this very real and personal knowledge of Christ; this treasure that allowed me to endure and not be crushed. And hopefully, as it poured out through my response to my mammoth disappointment, God could be glorified and hearts could be reached.

Back at the processing in San Francisco, I had chosen to have 'Proverbs 16:9' engraved on my Olympic ring. At the time, I thought that verse, "A man's heart plans his way, but the Lord directs his steps," encapsulated my journey to the Olympics. In my heart, as a fifth grader, I had dreamed of being an Olympic soccer player. And after 23 years of waiting and changing from soccer to running to mountain biking to road cycling, I had become an Olympian in a way that only God could have scripted. But now, and again only as God could have designed, Proverbs 16:9 also summarized the actual event.

My heart had dreamt of a medal, and I was physically ready to achieve it, but the steps the Lord had ordered for me were not standing on the podium. Instead, they had me standing on the side of the road while the dream washed away. As Proverbs 3:5-6 says, "Trust in the Lord with all your heart, and lean not on your own understanding; in all your ways acknowledge Him, and He shall direct your paths." I did not understand, but I trusted in the context of my default setting, and who I knew God to be.

In addition to the faith aspect of life, I also had to do what champions in every form of life do: Respond. Wallowing and being depressed about what

---

2. Job 42:2-3.

3. 2 Corinthians 4:7-8.

could have been in the road race or *should have been* in the time trial[4] would not do me any good. Instead, I controlled my attitude and my response. I drew the positive out, I learned from the negative, and I chose to turn my focus to the World Championships just seven weeks away. There was still time to rest from the Olympics and fight to win a set of "rainbow stripes,"[5] and there was still expectation in my heart for what God was capable of doing.

---

4. There was disappointment in not being selected to the cycling time trial race. I believed the Beijing time trial course would fit my strength as a rider since it had a gradual, long climb in it. I also had defeated the rider chosen instead of me head-to-head in every race over the last two years since the 2006 World Championships, where she had medaled. Obviously, the selection committee at USAC thought differently than I did, and since one piece of the selection criteria involved medaling at the 2006 World's race, I could see what led to their decision. I made a decision to let go of any fight for the time trial spot in favor of team harmony, out of respect for her, and with her promise of the world championship position later in the year.

5. The world champion wears a white jersey with a distinct set of stripes: blue, red, black, yellow, and green. Then, for the rest of that rider's career, she is allowed to wear the same stripes on the sleeve of her regular jersey. This designates the rider as a former world champion.

CHAPTER 9

THE LITTLE RED-HEADED GIRL IS A WORLD CHAMPION!

Having a God Focus in a Giant World

1 Samuel 16:7
But the Lord said to Samuel, "Do not look at his appearance or at his physical stature, because I have refused him. For the Lord does not see as man sees; for man looks at the outward appearance, but the Lord looks at the heart."(NKJV)

1 Samuel 17:37
Moreover David said, "The Lord, who delivered me from the paw of the lion and from the paw of the bear, He will deliver me from the hand of this Philistine." (NKJV)

1 Samuel 17:45-46a
David said to the Philistine, "You come against me with sword and spear and javelin, but I come against you in the name of the Lord Almighty, the God of the armies of Israel, whom you have defied. This day the Lord will deliver you into my hands..." (NKJV)

I returned home from Beijing exhausted. I had experienced the massive highs of the Olympic Games and becoming an Olympian; two things that could never be taken away from me. I had also faced extreme disappointment in not achieving what I had set out to do. In reflecting on everything, I realized that the value from a medal still would not have outweighed the value that came out of the process of chasing the dream.

The process developed relationships, created a daily grind that brought daily rewards, taught me how to handle victory as I achieved some goals (and defeat as I missed others), and it brought spiritual, mental, and physical growth to me through facing and overcoming adversity. I was extremely thankful for what God had given me through it all. I was doing what He made me to do, and He had me where He wanted me. So even though I was exhausted, I was able to balance it with this understanding. And to tweak a quote from Eric Liddell, "I know God made me fast, and when I 'ride' I feel His pleasure."[1]

Through it all, I also recognized that being a Christ-follower meant I had to be ready for God to take me places that I did not always expect. Perseverance, patience, and effort would be required in abundance. God's strength and wisdom was a necessity. There were no 'easy' buttons, and the giants of discouragement, impossibility, and my own inadequacy always loomed nearby. If I was going to continue to succeed after the Olympic Games, a very intentional God focus in every aspect of my life would be required.

So after I rested and pressed reset, I locked my eyes on Christ like a fighter pilot missile locks on a target. I also dialed in my vocational focus to the World Championship Time Trial. I had seven weeks, and I trained with determination, intelligence and a quiet ferocity. I was on another race mission, and I was motivated.

For the final two weeks of preparation, I went to Europe to do a block of racing that included seven races in eight days: A time trial in Italy, a five day stage race in Ardeche, France, and another one-day time trail in the northeast part of France. My goals were to ride hard and strictly to use these races for training. However, I managed to be in the top three in each time trial, and I won the

---

1. Lidell actually said "run" not ride. When we do what God made us uniquely and specifically to do, we will always feel his pleasure. It will not always be easy, but we will be moving in step with Him and be filled with a joy dependent on Him and not our circumstances.

Tour of Ardeche! At the end of this block my legs were cooked,[2] but this was expected, and I was exactly where I wanted to be.

I was 10 days out from the World Championship Time Trial—the perfect number of days to recover, get a response from this last work, and then refine my body for its peak event. During the first seven days, I stayed alone in Varese, Italy, in a hotel located on the time trial course. The peacefulness was a blessing. The introvert in me appreciated the quiet time. It allowed me to recharge my mental and social batteries while my body was recovering, and it gave me plenty of uninterrupted time to hang out with the Lord.

In addition to being missile locked (like a fighter pilot locks onto a target) onto the World's title, I was becoming 'missile locked' on Christ in a way that I never had before. I found myself reading the book "Facing your Giants," by Max Lucado, and spending a lot of time thinking about David and Goliath and praying about how to have a conquering faith. I decided I would do everything I could on my end, and then I would trust that where I was inadequate, God would fill in the details as He chose to do. I knew He wanted to do immeasurably more than anything I could imagine,[3] and I didn't want to get in the way. I yielded my life and trusted. There was definitely something special going on during that time. God was really close, and things were very clear for me.

On the bike, my alone time in Varese gave me a week to "recon" the time trial race course. I rode it over and over, forwards and backwards. I wanted to absorb every detail of each kilometer. I wanted my legs to understand what each felt like, where things rolled easy or hard, and where the *road feel* matched or did not match the *visual feel*. Along with the recovery and the recon that I was doing, I also needed to complete two motorpace sessions.[4]

Thankfully, my Aussie friend and Christian sister Vicky lived with the Australian team in the area and helped connect me with their director, Warren

---

2. Cooked. Stick a fork in me, I am done. Extremely fatigued.

3. Ephesians 3:20.

4. Motorpacing is a very specific workout where I ride an inch or two from the bumper of a motor-bike or a small car in a very big gear with a very high cadence at a high speed. The workout develops the neuromuscular firing patterns of pushing a big gear at a high cadence, while it also simulates race pace or more.

McDonald, aka Wazza. Wazza exhibited the sportsmanship that you find often within the women's side of cycling. He knew I was alone and needed help, and he made time to motorpace me twice. Those workouts were critical to my regeneration and final preparation, and looking back, I smile as I see God working there.

After my week alone, it was time to meet up with the USA team in Mendrisio, Switzerland, a small town on the other side of the Italian border but still very close to Varese. I had two remaining objectives during the final three days. The first was doing one additional hard motorpace session on the course to complete my prep work on the bike. The second was mentally locking in every detail of the course.

I had already started doing this while I was alone in Varese, but now it was time to get it completely dialed. I used the 'Official Training' ride, where the course was closed to traffic and the riders could see the course as it would look on race day, to take a video of it. All the way around the 25 kilometer course, I held onto my bike with one hand, and I used my camera to take a video with the other. Now I could use the video to ride it a hundred times in my head while I imagined what it would feel like to suffer and push through it. With the video, I could also visualize myself riding the technical portions, and I could nail down a pacing strategy for the race—two critical details to winning.

The morning of the race, I tried to stay calm and save my energy. I also did my best to eat just enough so that I was fueled, but I didn't have anything undigested in my stomach when it was time to ride. I did more visualization, lots of praying, and I spent some final time with David and Goliath. This time in an audio Bible study from Charles Stanley that was actually his online study for that day.

For some reason, I kept coming back to that story. It fit my situation perfectly. I was the little red head that was not the obvious pick to win or medal, and I was small in stature. In fact, I was the type of rider that most people assumed would never be able to time trial well. I was just too small and would never be able to produce enough power to win a world championship, so I was facing a challenge that may have looked impossible to the outside world. But just like David, I never saw the giant. I was only seeing God, and I went to the race with my stones in my pocket.

For my pre-warm up, I turned on some quiet music, and I took my bike for a walk. I did not want to ride the entire 25 kilometer race course, but I did want to see what the first part looked like when it was barricaded. I also wanted to settle on the exact effort level I would use for the beginning of the race. It was a fine line. I didn't want to go out too hard and have to recover from the start effort, but I needed to go out hard enough not to lose the race. I still remembered "eight seconds" and how every second counted.

After I scoped this out, I returned to the USA team tent and shifted into race hype-mode. I changed the music, but I maintained the zone of focus. I got on a stationary trainer to continue my warm up and to start riding hard. I gradually increased my intensity until I had taken my heart rate over my race pace level. I needed to get my body ready for the demands of the maximum 33 minute and 51 second effort that was to come, and my structured warm up turned on all of the necessary physiological systems. When I was finished, I was ready. Soon, it was "GO" time.

I pulled up my skinsuit, put on my helmet, and moved to the starting area. Here, I would have a few last minutes to get my mind ready and my butterflies in the right formation. Two minutes before my race time, I stepped onto the start ramp with confidence and peace knowing I was prepared. I had done the work. One minute before, I got onto the bike while a man held it steady and in place. As I waited for the clock to count down, I was still in this zone that I had never experienced. I took some deep belly breaths and said a last prayer. I was going to battle in the name of the Lord God Almighty, just like David. I think I smiled…and then…3beep, 2beep, 1beep, GO! I was off.

I paced the race perfectly. I hit the first climb with ideal rhythm and power. I was floating. I was doing everything I had visualized. Soon I hit the technical section that I had ridden more times in my head than on the bike. I flowed through it easily. Then I hit the middle section where I knew the race could be won or lost. I stayed focused. My head was on every single pedal stroke. There was nothing else going on in it except what I was doing in that exact moment. As I crested the last climb, I remember taking in the scene. There were lots of people on both sides, and I thought to myself, if I am going to win, I want to remember this. After that section, I entered the last third of the course, a slightly downhill road back to the finish. I stayed as aerodynamic as I could, and I disregarded all of the visual cues that my brain was getting. I knew it looked like we were going downhill, but based on what I had figured out in training, it was actually still a heavy rolling part of the course. I needed to work harder than it appeared I would. I stayed exactly in the moment, one pedal stroke at a time.

I made the final right turn and saw the "500M to go" sign. I pushed up the little bump with every last ounce of power as I focused on the finish line. Snot and slobber were flying off my face. I pedaled all the way across the line unaware of where I stood in the overall standings. As I was catching my breath, the race officials grabbed me. I had the fastest time! However, there were still 13 riders on the course.

I knew that I had just had the race of my life. Everything was aligned. My preparation in the final two weeks was perfect. And on race day, my legs, my lungs, my head and my heart all worked better than ever. Never had every piece of the puzzle worked together like that on the same day. It was a true world championship ride.

As I waited and watched from the hot seat, I was very guarded. I knew that all of the best riders had yet to finish, so it was very possible that my time would not last. However as one by one each finished, including the defending world champion and Olympic champion, I was still the fastest! I had won! I was the 2008 WORLD TIME TRIAL CHAMPION!!! Goliath went down hard.

I stood on the podium in my "Rainbow Stripes[5]" while the National Anthem played, and tears of joy and thankfulness poured out of me. I was overwhelmed by emotion as I reflected on my journey. I saw a lifetime of never giving up—and embracing adversity. I thought of all of the workouts I did that no one witnessed; the daily suffering, the daily commitment, the mental fortitude and resilience in the midst of all of it. I thought of my husband's unconditional love and support through our marriage, my cycling coach's dedication to help me be my best, and my high school and college coaches' guidance in my early spiritual development. I remembered my family's love and my mom

5. The World Champion is awarded a white jersey with blue, red, black, yellow, and green stripes on it. The year after winning the title the reigning world champion races in this jersey. Then, in all following years, stripes are worn on the sleeve to designate a former world championship.

teaching me as a youth soccer player that the word "cannot" did not exist. And most overwhelming of all was the depth of my relationship with Christ. He was the source of my strength, determination, and power, and I would not be there without Him. As I stood there, I felt his pleasure, and I couldn't stop the tears from flowing.

I also felt like the little red-headed girl who had focused on God's abilities and conquered the giant. During the previous seven weeks, I had intentionally tried to emulate David's vision in my quest. David was never concerned with Goliath's challenge or with Goliath himself. Instead, he always only saw God. He could have been discouraged by what he lacked in age, size, or appearance. He could have worried about not having the armor to protect him; or that his sling shot and five stones would be useless; or how easily he could have been mentally defeated by the size and strength of Goliath. But David knew the secret to success. To David it was simple. His inadequacies were easily covered by God's power and unlimited abilities. It wasn't about David. The battle with Goliath was God's responsibility, just like it was in David's previous victories against the lions and the bears. His heart discerned that nothing could succeed against the armies of the Living God of Israel, and that knowledge gave him the confidence he needed to face his giant and take the victory.

Like David, in my preparation, I had fixed my eyes on Christ and tried to eliminate all of the outside distractions or discouragement. I had yielded my life to His purposes, and my heart was seeking Him above all. I refused to see my own limitations or how improbable it would be for me to win. Instead, I only saw God's power and strength, and I continued to recall his previous victories with me. A world championship was certainly possible, but ultimately, the consequences were in God's hands. I locked my focus on Christ, took control of what I could with my physical preparation, and trusted He would do what was best.

When it was finally time for me to race the world championship, I went with the tools God had given me and with a determination to ride in His name. And for the first time ever, I also went with a confidence that the battle had already been won in prayer during my preparation. My remaining responsibility was to maintain my God focus, so I wouldn't be distracted by the giants looming around me. The day wasn't about me; it was about what God could do. And when it was over, I was the world champion.

I left Varese, Italy, excited to see what was next. The victory and the title would bring attention and opportunity for me to share my story—and to ultimately share God's story in my life. It also meant that I would get to race the 2009 season as the World Champion, a huge honor, and a very special thing in the sport of cycling.

Going forward, I wanted to continue the process of being the person God wanted me to be, while trying to achieve those goals He had helped me set. I knew, though, that I had to keep my eyes on Him as the giants and obstacles to His plans and purposes always seemed to reappear.

And when it came to what was next, I had no idea how hard things were going to get.

Chrono des Nations 2011. Time Trialing to victory.

*The 2005 Tour de l'Aude: Fanjeaux Finish. Stage Victory and my
first ever Yellow Jersey. (Photo Credit: Velopalmares)*

The 2005 Tour de l'Aude: Mijanes Finish. It was an epic fight to hold onto the yellow jersey; cold, wet, completely emptied, and victorious by 0.01 seconds. (Photo Credit: Velopalmares)

Jason and I at a Seattle Seahawks game in 2006.

Racing to the Team Trial Victory at the 2006 Route de France.

GP Roeselare Victory Salute. (Photo Credit: CJ Farquharson)

Jason and I in the Beijing Olympic Village.

Visiting with Jason outside the Beijing Olympic Village.

My guests for a day inside the Beijing Olympic Village. L to R:
Jason, my sister-Brooke, me, and Jason's sister-Amy.

At the Beijing Olympic Road Race: My sister and my husband with the flag.
My sister-in-law, Amy, in the background.

At the 2008 Beijing Olympic's Road Race: My sister Brooke, her husband Clint, their friend Lanie, and my husband Jason. Amy (Jason's sister) is taking the picture.

To Amber Neben
With best wishes,

President George W. Bush and I (middle) with some of the
USA track cyclists and staff around us.

The 2008 World Championship in Varese, Italy. Start Ramp. (Photo Credit: Stevens Bicycles)

The 2008 World Championship in Varese, Italy. Finish Stretch. (Photo Credit: Stevens Bicycles)

On the top step of the podium as the newly crowned world champion.

2008 Chrono des Nations: Wearing the world championship rainbow stripes for the time.

Jason and I in London just outside the Olympic Village.
Only athletes were allowed in the village.

The USA Olympic Road Race Team. London 2012. L to R: Evelyn, Kristin, Amber, Shelley

Jason doing his best ESPN College Game Day imitation during the London Olympics' Road Race live television broadcast.

The finish line of the 2012 London Olympic Games Time Trial. (Photo Credit: John Leyba/ Denver Post)

After the 2012 Olympic Time Trial race. L to R: My sister and my mom.

The rest of my 2012 cheering squad. L to R: Jason, Brooke, and Clint (Brooke's husband).

Leading the break in the 2012 World Championships Road Race. (Photo Credit: Bryn Lennon)

A 2013 Dare To Be Project **event at the Boys and Girls Club near Redlands, CA.**

*Rachel and I sharing a special hug after the 2012 World
Championships road race. (Photo Credit: Kramon)*

Motorpacing: Jason is driving the scooter, I'm on the bike, and my coach, Dave, is in the car checking on me. My riding speed in the picture is 47mph.

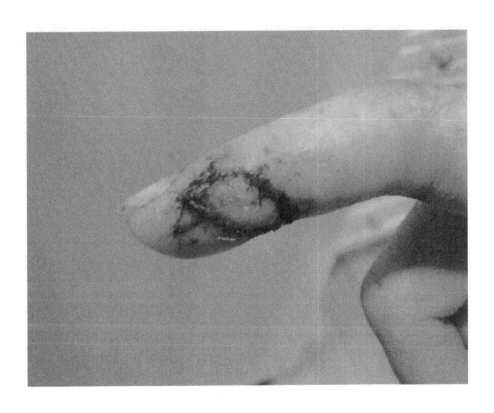

My right pointer finger about ten days after skin graft surgery
in July 2009. Courtesy of Dr. Karen Heiden.

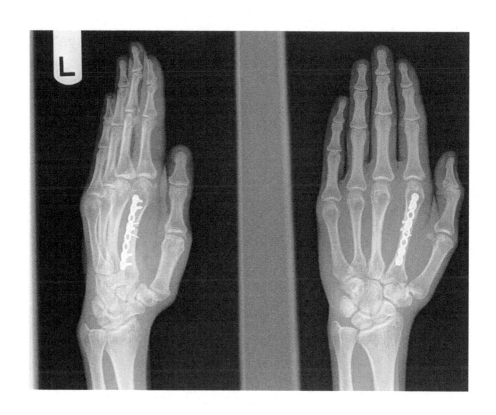

*My rebuilt left 2nd Metacarpal bone. Courtesy of Dr. Karen Heiden
in September 2009. Seven screws and one metal plate.*

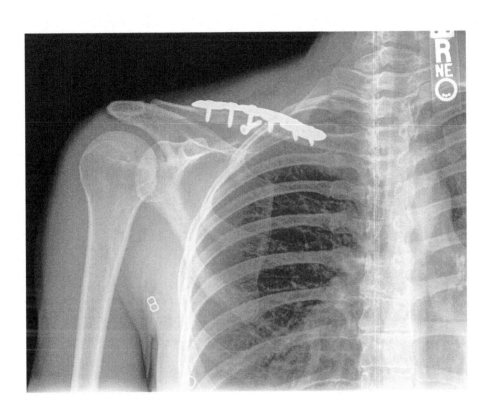

My rebuilt right collarbone. Courtesy of Dr. Eric Heiden in July 2010. Seven screws and one metal plate.

CHAPTER 10

FEAR

The First Two Times SHMACK Happened

Isaiah 41:10-13

So do not fear, for I am with you; do not be dismayed, for I am your God. I will strengthen you and help you; I will uphold you with my righteous right hand. For I am the Lord your God who takes hold of your right hand and says to you, 'Do not fear; I will help you.'

Joshua 1:9

Have I not commanded you? Be strong and courageous. Do not be afraid; do not be discouraged, for the Lord your God will be with you wherever you go.

Fear gripped me as I skidded to a stop against the guardrail and looked up at the entire peloton riding toward my head. Another rider had just slid into my front wheel, causing it to turn violently sideways, ripping the handlebars out of my hands, and instantly halting the bike's forward momentum. Since my body was still carrying the 30-plus mph speed and energy, I launched with my arms out like superman until I hit the pavement. Hard. The combination of the friction of my body on the road followed by the impact with the guardrail spun me around, so I could see what was coming at me. For a few seconds more, I was terrified of being run over until the peloton had passed.

After this immediate danger was gone, I realized my finger was screaming at me. I hadn't initially noticed it, but now it hurt like nothing I had ever felt. Fear grabbed me *again* as I connected the pain with the blood and the massive gash on it. I thought for sure I was going to lose the tip of it if I didn't get help fast.

I had no idea what had just occurred. We had crested a climb and started an easy downhill. I was still up front on the outside of the group. The corner was sweeping to the left, and I was looking far down the road...when suddenly I was tossed. It wasn't until later that night that the rider who was behind me explained what had happened, and why I had no chance to react or had any sense that it was coming.

I was in the middle of the 2009 racing season, coming off of the World Championship win the previous year. Only two days prior, I had won the time trial stage in this race, the women's Giro d'Italia. The win had catapulted me into the General Classification (GC) lead, and although I had cramped the next day and lost it, I was still close enough to fight back. There were enough hilltop finishes remaining, and I wasn't planning on giving up the race so easily. However, in an instant, everything changed. I went from being in contention, to being bloodied on the side of an Italian road in the middle of nowhere, waiting for the race ambulance and a doctor.

Eventually, help arrived and the medics came to assist me. One of them yanked my cycling glove off over the wound, creating even more pain. Meanwhile, the other one assessed my head and neck. Then, they put me on a gurney and jammed me into the back of the ambulance. As we traveled down the road, they tried to scrub off my wounds and figure out what else was wrong. I had deep cuts on my arms and elbows, while my quads and hip were also shredded. My left shoulder hurt badly too—but still, the finger was the worst.

We continued to drive, but since I was still in severe pain, the doctor asked the driver to stop so he could take a better look. He irrigated the finger again, examined it, and then stuck a needle directly into the wide-open gash causing me to yell out loud. He assured me amputation was not necessary. However, fear always draws us to the worst case, and my mind kept going there.

At that point, I had the option to stay with this doctor in the ambulance and follow the remainder of the race before going to an Emergency Room, or I could have gone with my team helper immediately. I opted to stay with the race ambulance. It meant that I had to endure bumping along in the back of the vehicle for two extra hours, but it guaranteed that I would have a doctor with me who spoke English. I didn't want to be alone. I didn't speak Italian, and let's be real; I was already scared.

Eventually we made it to an ER somewhere in southeastern Italy. First, I went to get X-rays on my shoulder[1] and finger. While I was going through this process, I prayed again for God to watch over me and hold me in His arms. I was afraid, and I needed Him to take care of me.

When the nurse returned to get me from the X-ray room, she told me that the doctor who happened to be on call was a hand specialist; actually, the only hand specialist in that region of the country. I started to cry. In the midst of the pain and chaos, there was God. Looking out for me. Reminding me that He had me in His hands. Telling me not to fear.

Back in the trauma area, the hand specialist blocked the nerve that inner-vated the damaged finger so that he could do exploratory surgery. Then, while

---

1. After the surgery, we X-rayed my shoulder again and figured out there was indeed a non-displaced fracture in the humeral head.

he operated, the nurse scoured my wounds with a scrub brush. I had slid across dirty, loose pavement, so I had a lot of small pebbles embedded in me in addition to the road rash. This cleaning process was very painful but necessary, and I did my best to lie still for the doctor.

When he finished the surgery, he explained that there was no damage to the tendon, but the nerve was partially severed and exposed. My finger would eventually be fine, but I would need a skin graft surgery to replace the section that was missing, and another surgeon would have to do that. He patched me up with bandages, and sent me on my way.

The next day, I flew from Rome to Park City, Utah, instead of home. It made the most sense since the long-time orthopedic doctors that I had consulted with throughout my career lived and worked there. In addition, my little sister lived in Park City and could take care of me until I made it home to my husband.

I promptly met with Dr. Karen Heiden, the hand and elbow specialist. She needed to see and assess the wound before she could schedule surgery. I still vividly remember that meeting, because the bandages were stuck. Her famous last words were, "I'm just going to rip it off like a Band-Aid." You can imagine what that felt like.

After seeing the damage, she made a plan to take an elliptical section of skin from the underside of my wrist and use it to sew a covering over the wounded area. It was possible that the graft would not stick permanently, but it would stay on long enough for new skin to safely grow underneath. It had to be done, so we scheduled surgery for the next day.

The procedure went well, and I recovered for two weeks in Park City. As I dealt with the crash and its ramifications, I got another chance to do what I do well: embrace adversity.

And soon enough, I was back to work on the bike. The World Championships were about two months away and within my reach. I still believed I could defend the title, and I wanted to race. I used all of my mental and physical toughness to prepare.

Unfortunately, as bike racing can go, I didn't have my best race on the actual day of the time trial. I hit my peak one or two days early, and on race day, my legs were really flat and lifeless. I was only good enough to be 7th. Although I was disappointed, I put it behind me. I wanted to be ready to do a good job for team USA in the World Championship Road Race that would take place just two days later.

Almost halfway through this 124-kilometer race, everything was still going according to the plan our director had laid out the night before. I had good legs again, and I was excited and in the moment. I was riding near the front where I could patrol and follow the riders I needed to follow. Then, as we started to enter a big, looping right turn, I backed off the wheel in front of me. The road was damp, and I wanted to give myself a little extra room to react.

Sure enough, the first rider slid out and crashed and then the second rider did the same. I was the third in line, and I was about to be next. However, in that split second the super slow motion button was pressed, and I weighed my options. I could lay the bike down and slide out with the other two girls, or I could try to go wide around them and head off course. Because the Giro crash and surgery were fresh in my mind, my brain chose the latter. But as I tried to go wide, I realized that this corner had metal barricades. I knew exactly what was about to happen.

I tucked my body the best that I could, but my left hand caught one of the vertical bars of metal. All of the force of impact went into my hand, followed by my head, and then the rest of my body. I rolled over on the pavement in extreme pain. The USA team car stopped briefly to get my status, but then the director had to continue following the race. I was left alone,[2] laying in pain on the road as I waited for the ambulance and race medics. This time, my hand was screaming, and my index finger was pointed sideways. It looked and felt bad. Thankfully, my head and neck were ok, but pain and fear gripped me again.

Here I was in an ambulance headed to an ER in a foreign country unsure of what was happening, or how bad I was hurt. Didn't I just do this? I didn't like being in pain, but the fear of not knowing what was wrong—and of being

---

2. There were a few race officials there, but I was alone in the sense that I didn't know anyone or understand the language.

in a hospital where I could not communicate with the doctors, my husband, or anyone back home—was worse. As I laid on the gurney in the back of the ambulance, I prayed for God to hold me and watch over me once again. I asked for His wisdom in understanding what was going on, and I tried to focus on Him. I tried to envision His right hand literally holding me.

After a long wait in the hospital, the US doctor who spoke Italian finally arrived to help me make some decisions. First, we would not move my finger and the bones attached to it before splinting my hand. Since there was a section of the second metacarpal that had been completely displaced, surgery and hardware were required, and there was no reason to endure the pain of setting things at this time. Second, it was not necessary to have surgery immediately, so I decided to fly back to the States for the operation. I wanted to be in a familiar environment.

The next day, instead of going home, I flew directly to Park City to see the same doctor who had fixed my finger. Again, she did an amazing job. This time she rebuilt the second metacarpal with a metal plate and multiple screws, realigned the finger associated with it, and got all of the tendons and ligaments in the right places. It was a very meticulous, two-hour surgery, but my hand would be fully functional after rehab.

The good news was that I was entering the offseason, so I would not miss any racing. The bad news was that I did have to recover from another surgery and another traumatic crash. And those take major physical and mental tolls on the body.

What a crazy final two and a half months of the racing season! It certainly wasn't how I envisioned finishing out my world championship season. However, despite how it ended, I still had much to be thankful for. I had a good first half of the year,[3] and I had managed to make a major comeback to try to defend the world championship. I also had faced real fear for the first time in my life, and watched God bring me through it.

I thought of Joshua, a man of faith who God equipped to conquer Canaan, but who also had to be reminded not to fear. During Joshua's equipping process, he saw that as Moses prayed and lifted his arms, success on the battlefield fol-

---

3. As the reigning world champion, I had won every time trial I had entered until the crash.

lowed.[4] Victory was a direct result of depending on God. Joshua clearly saw God working. Then, Joshua actually got to see God when He revealed himself to the elders (and Joshua[5]), giving him a very clear vision of who this God was. Joshua had firsthand knowledge and experience that should have eliminated any reason for him to fear as he moved forward doing what God wanted him to do.

However, God knew better—and in Joshua 1, when He gave Joshua his task as the new leader of Israel, He told Joshua to be strong and courageous three times in a span of five sentences. In fact, the last time he adds, "Have I not commanded you? Be strong and courageous. Do not be terrified; do not be discouraged, for the Lord your God will be with you wherever you go." And as Joshua progressed through Canaan, before the battle of Ai, before he fought the five Amorite kings, and before he went against the kings of the north, God reminded Joshua over and over, "Do not be afraid," He would fight for them.[6]

It was similar for me. All of a sudden, life was hard AND scary. I needed God to tell me over and over, *"Do not fear, for I am with you; do not be dismayed, for I am your God. I will strengthen you and help you; I will uphold you with my righteous right hand...For I am the Lord your God who takes hold of your right hand and says to you, Do not fear; I will help you."*[7]

Not only was I facing adversity, but I was also facing fear while things seemed to be getting more difficult. The opposition in my life continued to build as I drew closer to God and as I tried to reflect Him and carry out His purposes. I definitely knew who God was and what He was capable of doing, but I still desperately needed His reassurance as my fears stared me down.

Whether I was laying helpless on the side of the road, in the ambulance, or in the emergency room, those fears kept trying to crush me and change my focus. But each time as I faced them with my eyes turned toward God, He would bring me through the situation. Then, with every advance, my ability to be courageous and to stand firm grew stronger, and the fear dissipated faster. God

4. Exodus 17:10-11.
5. Exodus 24:9-13.
6. Joshua 8:1; 10:8; 11:6.
7. Isaiah 43:10,13.

was responding and adding to the faith and understanding He had already built into my life. Now, even though the fear was there, it did not have power over me. Instead, I could feel that mighty right hand holding me tight, and I could hear God's promises to be with me and to fight for me.

"Do not fear. Do not be discouraged. Be strong and courageous. I am with you wherever you go. I will not forsake you. I am your God. I will fight for you." All of God's promises to Joshua and his people were also for me.

I wrote these on my heart. I would need them.

CHAPTER 11

PRESSING ON AND DISCERNING THE RACE SET BEFORE US

Another Crash and Another Piece of Hardware

Hebrews 12:1b-2
...and let us run with endurance the race that is set before us, looking unto Jesus, the author and finisher of our faith, who for the joy that was set before Him endured the cross...(NKJV)

Philippians 3:13-14
...But one thing I do: Forgetting what is behind and straining toward what is ahead, I press on toward the goal to win the prize for which God has called me heavenward in Christ Jesus.

Ending up in an ambulance, then an emergency room in a foreign country, and then surgery on two separate occasions during a three-month
period in 2009—as a direct result of cycling—certainly made me take
a hard look at what I was doing. I had been through enough in life to know I
should take a step back and ask God if He was trying to show me something
to change in my life, give me a task, or have me consider if it was time to move
on from cycling. On the other hand, it was also possible that the latest obstacles
were simply the opposition trying to discourage me. But first it was important
to look inward. Over my years of walking with Christ, I had discovered this.
Of course, obstacles in life weren't always about the condition of my heart, but
if it was, I wanted to start the process earlier rather than later. But as I prayed
and thought about these questions, I kept coming back to Paul and his Biblical
parallel of a running race to the race of life.

As an athlete, I easily related to his analogy, and I pondered how hard it was
to ride (or run) a race. I knew very well that to race and finish strong required
preparation. I also knew that to continue to do it required ongoing training. It
was impossible to work out for only one day...and then expect to be competitive
for the rest of the year. No. I needed to be disciplined on a daily basis; to train
hard and stay focused on my goals. And as I put in this time and effort, my
ability to compete (or "endure" as Paul would say), would improve. And then, if
I could continuously be patient, persevere, maintain perspective, and pay attention to the details, I could be successful.

This progression was rarely easy, though. In fact, intense workouts challenging me to fight hard and be uncomfortable for brief periods of time were
an ongoing requirement during the season. They were essential in developing
and maintaining my cardiovascular, muscular, and mental endurance. Without
them, I would not be able to finish a race strong. Of course, throughout the year,
it was also very normal for me to have a bad workout or fail with some compo-
nent of training. But when things would go wrong, I was flexible and adapted
quickly, or I simply let it go and kept moving forward. I kept my focus on the
goal and refused to be discouraged. Finally, there were many days when I was
tired and weary, but I still had to train.

Knowing all of that, I appreciated Paul's attempt to use athletics and racing as a metaphor for life. The parallels were intriguing to me, and God kept

bringing me back to these passages as I contemplated my future in the context of my recent crashes. He also kept reminding me of Paul's life and his struggles. Soon I heard God telling me to keep going and not to quit this race that he had set before me. I heard him tell me that I needed to press on and to run with endurance. I was broken, but I was not deterred. I would stay in the "race."

As I recovered from hand surgery in October of 2009, I signed a new contract with the same team, and I set goals for the next season. However, it only took two months for the first roadblock to appear. In late December, the team lost its sponsorship, and I was left without a team *and* without a salary.

My best option was to look to the USA national team to find racing, and it turned out to be a big blessing. For many years, I had been competing in Europe with Europeans only, but now I had a chance to give back and share from the storehouses of my own experiences with the young American superstars. I had learned a lot along the way, and the idea of being able to mentor the next generation was appealing.

Our season started fast and well. We raced the Tour of New Zealand in February of 2010, and Team USA won all of the stages and the overall title. It was exciting to work with such a dynamic and cohesive group, and it energized me for the future.

I was set to race the April Spring Classics in Europe next. But two days before the first race, my bike was lost by the airlines, and I had to ride the Tour of Flanders (the first of these Classics), on equipment that was not my own. I ended up tearing my rectus femoris and adductor longus, two major muscles in my quad and hip flexor, and I had to sit out for the next five weeks. Recovery required total rest and that meant a total loss of fitness! I was disappointed. It was another road block.

But I PRESSED ON, and I refused to give up. I had to be patient and endure the process of retraining my body and restoring my level of strength while I was also racing. It was not ideal, and it did not happen as fast as I would have liked, but slowly I gained ground.

It started with the National Championships in late June, where I was able to fight for a second place result. Then, I continued to work hard on my own, so that I would be good enough to help my USA team and our rising climbing superstar, Mara Abbott, target the Giro d' Italia in July. Although I wasn't at my best, I was still capable of contributing and playing a role. It was rewarding for me to be a background servant, even if it meant returning to the race where I almost ripped my finger off the year before.

In fact, I had almost completed the 2010 version of the race. We had finished seven out of nine days of racing, and Mara had been the class of the field dominating in the mountains and setting herself up to win the overall title. I was also finally feeling better on the bike as my race fitness had improved with each stage. Things were going very well now, and the rest of my season looked promising.

But on that second to last day of racing, I was in another wreck. This time, it was very horrific. We were descending down a straight but very steep road at about 55mph. I was riding in about 5th position, right behind my teammate Amanda Miller, in what should have been a perfectly safe spot. However, sometimes people do stupid things, and one rider tried to squeeze past Amanda where there wasn't enough room. She contacted Amanda's handlebars, and the next thing I knew, both of them were crashing right in front of me. My 'slow motion' button was pushed again, and the chaos, carnage, and exit strategies all played out in front of me.

I could see that going to the right or to the left was not possible. Either their bodies or their bikes were flying across the road. My last and only option would be to try to bunny hop over everything. But as this was going through my mind, I realized the bikes floating in front of me were too high. I must have blacked out around that moment, because I don't remember the impact.

The next day, I learned that one of the flying bikes actually sawed my own fork and wheel in half. It literally cut through everything while I was on the bike moving at more than 50mph. My body was flung directly downward onto my right shoulder and head, and then I tumbled and skidded across the road until I came to a stop.

Thankfully, I don't remember those details, but I did remember being sprawled out on the pavement in severe pain while Amanda's tattered body stood over me. She was asking me if I was okay and could keep going. But I was too hurt to move, so obviously there was no way I would be able to get back on the bike.

Soon, I was in an ambulance following a race in Italy on my way to a *still to be determined* emergency room. Sigh. We eventually found one. But since it didn't have an X-ray machine, they bounced me out, and then back into the ambulance for no reason. We immediately started driving again, and after another hour, we finally found a hospital that had a modern touch to it.

Then, on the X-ray table, it was typical Italy. The two technicians argued with each other as they each pulled on separate jersey sleeves. I was screaming for them to stop, because I knew something was broken in my shoulder or collarbone area, but they kept yanking. The lady actually told me to "shut up" in perfect English. I motioned to her with my hand to use scissors to cut off the jersey. "How hard is that?" I thought. I wanted to motion something else, but I refrained, and she proceeded to cut off ALL of my clothes, take the x-rays, and then leave me laying naked on the gurney. Seriously.

I finally convinced her to put a sheet over me, but then she just left me in an empty, white walled hallway. At some point, a male nurse found me and wheeled me away for a doctor to do an ultrasound of my abdomen. Thankfully, there was nothing internally wrong, and I was moved to the next room for the tragic comedy to continue.

The X-rays were ready to be examined by the doctor. He entered the room and said a few words to me. Then, he held the fuzzy X-ray high up over his head so that the light above would illuminate it. He confirmed that I had a broken collarbone, strapped a figure-8 brace around me, looked at the huge puncture wound on my side, mumbled something in Italian, and then sent me away. Did that really just happen? Eventually, the team director arrived. We checked out of the hospital and drove a long way back to the hotel.

Two miserable days later, I was flying back to Utah again, but this time I would meet with Dr. Eric Heiden, the shoulder and knee specialist of the Heiden pair. He took new X-rays with a modern machine, and he could see that my collarbone was in pieces. I definitely needed a plate and screws for things to heal properly and quickly, so we scheduled surgery immediately.

During the latest ambulance ride and then through the months of recovery that followed, I had to ask again, "Was I really in the right race?" It seemed like things were continually working against me. Was I missing something? Was God simply speaking louder and louder to get my attention? I wrestled with what had happened—and whether I was doing what God wanted or what I wanted.

But just like the last times, God was still telling me to PRESS ON. Yes, He had set this race before me. It was His. He had marked it out for me, it was still the right one, and I still needed to endure it. However, I also needed to raise my level of perseverance.

Until the last two years, most of my previous adversity had allowed me to personally grow and equip me for my next steps. But these recent trials and tribulations seemed to be challenging something above me. God was using me, and I felt the opposition to His purposes getting stronger. Now, I realized how important it would be to do as Paul did when he said, "I PRESS ON to take hold of that for which Christ Jesus took hold of me. Brothers and sisters, I do not consider myself yet to have taken hold of it. But one thing I do: Forgetting what is behind and STRAINING TOWARD what is ahead, I PRESS ON toward the goal to win the prize for which God has called me heavenward in Christ Jesus."[1] And then again when he encouraged us to "run WITH PERSEVERANCE the race marked out FOR us, fixing our eyes on Jesus..."[2] Never before had these ideas been so clear, nor had I ever applied them to the big picture kingdom view of life.

Discerning all of this was not easy, but it was a result of being very persistent in my prayer life and in reading the Bible. I continually asked my own questions and listened for answers, but I also reminded God that I knew what He told me in Psalms:

I will instruct you and teach you in the way you should go, I will counsel you and watch over you (Ps. 32:8). *The plans of the LORD stand firm forever, the purposes of His heart through all generations* (Ps. 33:11). *The eyes of the LORD are on those who fear Him* (Ps. 33:18). *I sought the Lord and He answered me* (Ps. 34:4).

And in Jeremiah 29:12-13: *Then you will call on me and pray to me and I will listen to you. You will seek me and find me when you seek me with all your heart.*

And of course, my compass from Proverbs 3 to trust in the LORD with all my heart and lean not on my own understanding; in all my ways acknowledge him and He would make my paths straight.

---

1. Philippians 3:12-14.
2. Hebrews 12:1b-2a.

So I sought His guidance diligently, and I listened intently. And then I waited, and kept on waiting, until the voice was clear. When it was time to move, I would know. But until then, I had to be still, and I had to be persistent in prayer.

It took time. I had to be patient. I often wanted God to send me a text message or put the answer on a flashing billboard, but he would not and did not. I had to keep seeking Him with all my heart, be still and wait. I also had to block out the outside world, so that I could hear God's whisper and not be fooled by its distractions. After all, the world and Satan wanted me in the wrong race.

Eventually, the answer was very clear for me, and this time was the same as the last few. I needed to keep going and not quit. God wasn't done with me in the world of cycling, and I needed to continue pursuing the goals that He put on my heart. And I did.

Two months after surgery, I made it back to the World Championships (in Australia) in the middle of September. I finished 4th (a wood medal) in the time trial, and then I did a good job in the road race. I also signed a two-year contract with a big team and a familiar owner. It had been a hard 13 months, but in pressing on through it, I felt a great peace, and I knew God had me.

Although I was excited for the future, after this race I was also completely drained from the previous battles. Pressing on always required all of me mentally, physically, emotionally, and spiritually, and I was really feeling the strain after the last four events. Thankfully, the season was now over, and I could get some rest.

I walked out onto the Melbourne, Australia, beach at dusk and watched the sun set. I took in the power of the waves, the immense stretches of water, the infinite number of grains of sand, and I watched as the stars came out in bunches. There was my God and my default setting. The same God who numbered the grains and called out the stars, not only died for me, but still had me in His hands. I let go of everything that was behind, and I gave Him my future. It wasn't about me. It was about that one person who might see Jesus because of me. I HAD to keep pressing on and straining toward what was ahead.

The 2012 Olympic Games were only a year and half away, and if God wanted me there, He would get me there. However, as I felt His encouragement moving into 2011, I also sensed Him prompting me to be ready to stand firm and to keep my spiritual armor on. It would be essential.

CHAPTER 12

GETTING DRESSED FOR BATTLE

...and Finally, Encouraging VICTORIES!

Ephesians 6:10-11

Finally, be strong in the Lord and in his mighty power. Put on the full armor of God, so that you can take your stand against the devil's schemes.

Ephesians 6:14-18

Stand firm then, with the belt of truth buckled around your waist, with the breastplate of righteousness in place, and with your feet fitted with the readiness that comes from the gospel of peace. In addition to all this, take up the shield of faith, with which you can extinguish all the flaming arrows of the evil one. Take the helmet of salvation and the sword of the Spirit, which is the word of God. And pray in the Spirit on all occasions with all kinds of prayers and requests.

In the New Testament, James said, "Consider it pure joy, my brothers and sisters, whenever you face trials of many kinds, because you know that the testing of your faith produces perseverance. Let perseverance finish its work so that you may be mature and complete, not lacking anything."[1]

I certainly was far from being a finished product, but as I persevered through trial after trial, I was also gaining wisdom and growing in spiritual maturity. The storms had forced me to be in the Word, in prayer, and actively seeking and clinging to Christ. And in turn, He always responded to each by providing exactly what I needed, whether or not I realized it. Great was His faithfulness.

He was also the potter who held the pot (me) in His hand, and He kept turning the adversity into a tool to sculpt His beauty into me. It wasn't that my cancer, the crashes, or the other adversities were inherently good. Alone, they would have been terrible chapters in my life—and probably would have crushed me; but God continued to transform them into something good. I could see this. And as I did my best to consider it pure joy as I faced the onslaught of storms, He made me more complete and more like Him, including my perspective and my vision.

In fact, the most recent weather pattern had further opened my eyes to the spiritual opposition that was all around me. To paraphrase Paul in Ephesians 6, I needed to *"Put on the full armor of God, so that (I could) take (my) stand against the devil's schemes. For (my) struggle (was) not against flesh and blood, but against the rulers, against the authorities, against the powers of this dark world and against the spiritual forces of evil in the heavenly realms."* It wasn't a concept I heard preached about often, but as I drew near to Christ, and He used me more for His purposes, this big picture opposition and war I was in became more evident. Finally, I understood why it was so important to get dressed with my spiritual armor daily.

How to do it was the next question, and Ephesians 6:10-18 went on to explain this. I decided to add it to my daily wardrobe by using the technique of mental imagery to picture myself putting every piece of equipment on while I thought about what each represented.

I visualized myself putting on a helmet, my *helmet of salvation*. Jesus had already won. The battles would be daily, but the war was won on the cross, and

1. James 1:2-4.

112

I recalled this when I put on my helmet. I also asked God to guard my thoughts as I went through the day. Then, I envisioned myself putting on the *breastplate of righteousness*. Again because of what Christ had already done on the cross, I was justified and free of condemnation and could stand before Him. As I covered my heart with His righteousness represented by the breastplate, I asked Him to guard my emotions and give me the inner strength to live in a way that represented Him accurately. Next, I put on the *belt of truth*. I reminded myself that Jesus said, "I am the way the truth and the life."[2] I asked Christ to help me discern His voice, to be sensitive to His guidance through the truth of scripture, and to help keep my motives pure. Then there were the *shoes* of the *gospel of peace*. This time I told myself that I needed to stand firm on the hope and peace of the gospel. As I traveled through my day, this hope and perspective would keep me "standing firm" no matter what came at me. They would also keep me ready to share when I needed to. Then I envisioned myself picking up my giant *shield of faith* so that I could defend myself against the devil's tricks and darts. I was thankful that God had tested my faith, so I knew my shield could and would work. I grabbed my *sword* next. I asked God to bring His word to my mind in defense and in offense at the right times. Finally, I confirmed that I had to be strong in God's power and might and not my own.

Every day I did this. In the same way that I put on the correct jersey, shorts, shoes, and helmet, and then filled my pockets with food so that I could have a successful training day on the bike, I also began to put on my spiritual armor as preparation for succeeding in life's battles. It made sense to me.

So now, after my last stint of rehab, I was ready to get dressed to ride my bike outside and compete spiritually again, but I was also in need of some encouragement. Thankfully, God knew this already, and as I transitioned from this last period of my life into the next, He gave me reassurance in three different ways to keep me in the battle and to help me see the whole of it.

First there was the amazing peace I received after signing my next contract. At the end of 2010, I inked a two-year deal to ride for HTC-Highroad, the biggest women's team on the circuit—and one of the few women's teams run under

2. John 14:6.

a Men's PRO Tour team. Immediately, I was surrounded by the best riders, staff, equipment and ownership. It was truly a blessing that came out of waiting through all of August and then into late September to sign. I had felt pressure to choose a team earlier, but HTC-Highroad was not one of the original options. So each time I was close to making a decision, something in my spirit made me pause. And because I listened, I ended up with the best option, and I was filled with a tremendous amount of peace. It was confirmation that I made the right decision, and I was thankful that I waited. I was also extremely thankful for the encouragement that came with the peace.

Second, there were multiple cycling success stories that reminded me that my athletic goals were still within reach. In March, I won the first two races that I started with the team: the San Dimas Stage Race and the Redlands Classic in California. Then, on Easter Sunday, I won my first ever one-day Classic in Europe, the GP Stad Roeselere!

It was a big race in Belgium, but I didn't have any personal expectations; I only wanted to ride hard for the team. Because of that approach, I rode aggressively all day, trying to initiate a successful break. And for 110 out of 135 kilometers, everything failed. Then, with about 20 kilometers to go as we entered the final circuits around the town, the perfect moment for an attack presented itself. I recognized the opportunity, and I gave one last huge effort that allowed me to escape alone! Initially, I thought my attempt to get away would only be a tactical move that would put pressure on the other sprinter teams to work and close the gap to me. But as I rode, my strength and my gap remained steady, and I recalled my morning scripture and grew more confident.

I stayed away[3] and won! I crossed the finish line with the most joyful victory salute ever. Fittingly, Psalm 28:7 captured the moment perfectly: "The Lord is my strength and my shield; my heart trusts in him, and he helps me. My heart leaps for joy, and with my song I praise him." In addition, the verses from Ephesians where Paul talked about having access to the same strength that rose Christ from the dead, were also on my heart that Easter morning. I will forever remember the race, because my heart leapt for joy after I used that strength to win.

---

3. The term "stayed away" means to maintain the race lead ahead of the chasing peloton.

From Belgium, I went to Luxembourg, to Medellin, Colombia, to multiple places in the States, to Germany, Sweden, Italy, France, Denmark, and eventually back to France as the season continued. In country after country, my team kept winning, and I continued to taste success and feel more encouragement.

I earned another new victory in June at the Nature Valley Grand Prix, and then I claimed two more very close second places. I actually lost the National Championship Time Trial by 23/100 of a second, and then the Thüringen-Rundfahrt (a big seven-day race in Germany) by three seconds. But as the cliché goes, 'that is bike racing.' And although second place is always hard, these were two great podiums to add to everything else the team and I achieved throughout the year. In all, 2011 was fun both on and off the bike, and it was exactly the kind of season that I needed. Again, I was extremely thankful for the encouragement.

But most importantly, the year brought new reminders of the real reason that God had placed me in the sport. People. There were multiple connections and conversations with the people God was impacting through me, as a result of what I was doing as a Christian cyclist. All around me, there was still evidence that God was working, and His plans were not being thwarted. I WAS on track.

One example had occurred early in the season in March on the Saturday afternoon of the Redlands Classic. Normally, I wouldn't warm up on a stationary trainer unless I had a time trial. However, it was an important criterium, and that day I chose to do so with my teammates. This meant that instead of riding out on the local roads, I was under a tent riding in place.

While I was doing this, a father with his four daughters slowly and respectfully approached me. I could sense something special going on, so I stopped to interact. I found out they had driven more than two hours to specifically seek me out. I was honored, and I took time to write a note to each of the girls and then take a photo with them. I was thankful for the chance to share and for the "people" reminder of why I was doing what I was doing.

However, it wasn't until a few days later, after I received a powerful and humbling thank you email from their father, that I realized the magnitude of the visit. It gave me a glimpse of God working through me in a way I didn't initially see, and it confirmed to me that pressing on was right. God wasn't finished with me in the sport just yet.

115

All through the year, similar things happened as I made myself available for Him. I was able to share from the story He was writing in my life, and how He had worked through all the ups and downs. Then, because I was available, He could act. To get feedback that I had inspired peoples' lives was extremely encouraging! And interestingly, it also helped me to recognize that my battle was shifting from *medals* to *hearts*.

For most of my career, the battle was the medal, and as I fought and won, or fought and struggled, God worked through me in small ways. Yet as much as I wanted Him to use me and work through me in greater ways, and as much as I thought this was associated with winning more, He knew I wasn't ready for the first—and He had better ideas for the second. I won enough titles for Him to give me credibility and place me where I needed to be. Then, my adversity opened doors I wouldn't have imagined with others—while it also refined, shaped, strengthened and equipped me.

The process was uncomfortable and just plain hard at times, but in choosing to persevere, I learned that His grace was sufficient, His love was real, His power was awesome, and He wanted me to draw near to Him. Then, as I spent more time reading His word and praying, He came close to me and gave me His strength. My faith was tested and proved. I gained a big-picture perspective that helped me see things from His point of view, and I grasped WHO and how GREAT He is. All of those concepts in turn helped me to depend on Him, do what He asked me to do, and set goals that I could only accomplish with His help. Nothing was too hard for Him, and no detail of my life was too small. I also learned about patience, and how important it was to wait and obey even when it was difficult. My pride was often checked, too, to keep me alert to its subtle advances and the danger it presented to doing more.

Most importantly, though, the value and priority of doing everything in prayer first was drilled into me. When I wrestled against the principalities and powers, against the discouragement, the distractions, and blatant attacks, I needed to be in prayer. If I was going to keep on keeping on and not give up, I needed to persevere in prayer. I also needed to be inquiring of God often and seeking victories in prayer before the battles began. Prayer kept my confidence in God and not myself, and it was the secret to success—a vital part of my armor. It kept me depending on God and helped me stay in His will. If I stopped, I would fail.

All of that preparation took place while my focus was the battle for the medal. But during this last season, I sensed my primary battlefield shifting. I was far from complete, but I was prepared; and now, I sensed God making a change.

My main focus was no longer the medal, but the heart. I would absolutely still pursue "gold" with everything I had. Who God made me, what He had given me, and the goals He put on my heart had not changed. I very much wanted to be a good steward of those gifts, I was still very driven to succeed, and it was still possible that the medal could serve His purposes in amazing ways. However, as I stepped forward, dressed in my spiritual armor with the perspective and equipping that came as a result of my life's journey to this point, I understood that the medal was only a temporary achievement—while the changed hearts would last forever. And whatever the most effective way for Him to do that, was okay with me.

Hearts. People. Eternity. It was critical that I got dressed properly every day. Success would require me to stay strong in the LORD and the power of His might. The battle was ongoing.

It was ongoing for the medal, too. I was extremely motivated to go for Gold at the upcoming World Championships, and the London Olympics were calling me loud. I was riding very well, and I was filled with encouragement. I felt ready, and I had my ideas about both. But God always directed my steps, and as the selection seasons were about to begin, could I see Christ and only Christ, no matter what kind of chaos was around me?

CHAPTER 13

STANDING FIRM
WHILE GOD ORCHESTRATED

From 2011 World's Selection
to June 2012 Olympic Selection

John 15:5
I am the vine; you are the branches. If you remain in me and I in you, you will bear much fruit; apart from me you can do nothing.

Ephesians 6:13, 17
Therefore take up the whole armor of God, that you may be able to withstand in the evil day, and having done all, to stand...and take...the sword of the Spirit, which is the word of God. (NKJV)

Philippians 4:6
Do not be anxious about anything, but in every situation, by prayer and petition, with thanksgiving, present your requests to God.

As the 2011 season neared its end, I started my fight to be one of the four women selected for the Olympic Road Race—and one of the two selected for the Time Trial. I was dressed for battle in true Ephesians 6 style, but now I had to stand firm. When the enemy would challenge me with discouragement, distraction, anxiousness, worry, and more fear, standing firm enabled me to succeed. And when living for Christ was uncomfortable or might limit my opportunities, standing firm kept me courageous.

Fixing my eyes on Christ was part of it; but to really stand firm, I had to abide in Christ who said, "I am the vine, you are the branches. He who abides in Me, and I in him, bears much fruit; for without Me you can do nothing."[1] But to know how to abide, I had to recognize that the Vine was the Word. "In the beginning was the Word, and the Word was with God, and the Word was God."[2] If I was reading and absorbing Scripture, I would be abiding in Him. If I knew His word, I would know Him and how He worked. Then, when I was in the Word, its power to inspire, calm, strengthen, and lead would be unleashed.

As this biblical analogy became clear, I understood the subtleties of my role and how to stand firm. I never had to make the fruit or try to make the fruit. I didn't have to fight or stand firm in my own strength. I just had to stay attached to the vine so that His power and strength could flow through me and do the work. When the branch was attached to the vine, the sap from the vine would flow through it and produce fruit. In the same way, if I was abiding in Christ, the Holy Spirit could continuously flow through me and God would meet my needs through His Spirit. I would bear fruit as a byproduct of abiding IN Him. And IN Him, anything was possible! In contrast, apart from Him, I would be ineffective and fail.

As I made time to "abide," I also needed to stay focused and take care of the details of my training and preparation on the bike. I still had to be a good steward of my abilities, work hard, control my attitude, persevere, and stay on course. But when distractions or discouragements came my way, I practiced standing firm, and then in faith, let go of the consequences—knowing God would orchestrate according to His will and plans.

---

1. John 15:5.
2. John 1:1.

Almost immediately, during the Olympic selection season, a challenge to stand firm with regards to my 2011 World Championship time trial bid came up. This issue was important because it was the first opportunity to automatically qualify for the 2012 London Games. If I could win a medal by placing in the top three at the Worlds in late September in Copenhagen, then I would secure my start spot for the Olympics and remove any selection doubt that might predictably come up. There were no guarantees, but I had been focused on this race since January, and I had ridden well enough through the year to know that I was capable of a medal. I also knew I had done enough to earn the spot.

However, stunningly, I was not nominated to the time trial team. The decision was unexpected and somewhat baffling, and I thought an error had occurred. After I re-inspected the selection criteria, I confirmed that the selection committee did not properly apply USA Cycling's own published criteria. I had to act quickly on my own behalf, regardless of the potential emotional and/or career consequences. If I didn't stand now, I might lose my future chance at securing an Olympic spot.

With the help of my husband, Jason, I challenged the decision by following the process that USA Cycling (USAC) had established for such issues. It was a long shot, but it was the right thing to do. To our surprise, USAC actually agreed to hire an independent investigator to reassess the decision. He found the same problems and conflicts we did, and although he recommended that the selection committee be reconvened with a new independent coach to lead the discussion, USAC still had to accept this finding. Again, to our surprise, they did, and now, I had the opportunity to properly present my case.

The process demanded a lot of time and energy, and we spent days and nights (we were in Europe and eight hours ahead of Colorado) putting together the documents and data that showed why I deserved the spot according to the selection criteria. We chose not to hire an attorney, and instead, we prayed and used our common sense...or God's foolishness. After all, the foolishness of God is still wiser than man's wisdom.[3]

It was a very stressful time. First, it felt like there was a battle taking place to prevent me from doing what God wanted to do with me through cycling.

---

3. 1 Corinthians 1:25.

It was a battle that had nothing to do with the flesh and blood of USAC, but everything to do with what the apostle Paul described in Ephesians 6:12, and it was extremely draining. Second, the race was only two weeks away, and I was also emptying myself both physically and mentally in training as I prepared for the competition.

As the appeal process continued, I compartmentalized my activities. I had to force myself to shut off thoughts about the selection during training and recovery. Then, I had to quickly switch gears to focus back on the selection issue, so I could help Jason with paperwork or talk to related parties on the phone. Thankfully, Jason took on all of the work and stress of creating documents to present the data—which gave me more time to leave the details of my life to Christ through prayer. It was an intense time of being challenged to trust, stand firm, and not be anxious spiritually. I had to make a huge effort to only see Christ. Meanwhile, physically, I kept preparing as if I had the spot.

However, as much as Jason and I tried, we eventually got to the same point that King Hezekiah did back in Isaiah 37. Hezekiah's response happened after the King of Assyria, Sennacherib, had been on a rampage and proclaimed Israel next on the hit list. Sennacherib had sent warnings via messengers—and then a letter to King Hezekiah mocking him and his God and bragging about their own previous victories. Hezekiah was facing a genuine political threat, but he also knew he needed to stand firm. After receiving the letter, he literally spread it out before the LORD and said, "look at this and listen to what the Assyrians say!"[4] Then, he asked God to deliver them.[5]

In a strangely applicable way, Jason and I did the same. We did our research and got advice from the right people, but in the end, we just let it go. We put it back in God's hands. We laid our documents down on the table, told Him that He had to do this if He wanted it done, and then we trusted He would work according to His will. It probably wasn't the smartest strategy from the world's point of view, but we are not of this world.[6]

---

4. Isaiah 37:14.

5. Isaiah 36, 37.

6. John 17:14.

Then, something very rare happened. In fact, it is possible it has only occurred one other time. The selection decision was overturned. I had the spot and the chance.

I had chosen to stand firm instead of lying down, because there was enough evidence to fight the decision. It was the right thing to do. They had not followed their own criteria, and both the results of the investigator and the new committee proved that.

However, when I arrived a few days later to the American team's hotel base in Copenhagen, I felt very uncomfortable. I did my best not to let it bother me, but the negative energy from those around me (and the underlying tension) wiped me out. It was a terrible first night.

Eventually this tension eased, but it had already done its damage. On race day, I started well, but the second half of my race suffered, and at the finish, I was a distant and disappointing 7th place. The only positive was that I was still the top American and my Top-10 result qualified a second start position in the time trial for Team USA at the 2012 Olympic Games. Although I had done my best to stay focused in the midst of the chaos, my energy and spirit had been drained, and my focus *had* been shifted. I had tried to stand firm, but I was negatively affected.

Leaving Copenhagen, I reminded myself that God's bigger picture plan would not be stopped, and I needed to trust Him and make a bigger effort to stand firm and abide in Christ. I also flipped my perspective to view things through His eyes. I had wanted to be able to plan my training with the certainty of knowing that I was already on the Olympic team, but this result would keep me relying on Him and not myself. It would force me to keep seeking Him first. It was also a good motive check and reminder not to allow the allure of victory to pull me off course. Winning gold was good, but winning hearts for the Lord was better, and I knew God would do things His way.

This series of events with the world's selection actually started a pattern that I would continue to see as I worked toward London and the Olympics. There would be a challenge to surrender because something wouldn't go as I expected, or there were be an obstacle or subtle attempt by the enemy to discourage or distract me. I would proceed to stand firm, just as I had before, and then God would give me a glimpse of where I was headed with a reminder that said, "I have you. Trust me."

After my disappointing World's results, the first glimpse of God's direction came my way. I went to the far west of France for a one-day time trial, the Chrono des Nations. It was a chance for me to finish my season racing like I knew I was capable of doing. But unexpectedly, I also had the chance to go head to head against the same rider who had originally been selected ahead of me for the spot in Copenhagen—and was historically the best in the world. This detail added pressure, but it also meant that a victory would help me for the Olympic Time Trial selection, and it would vindicate my position in the recent selection debacle.

I won the race and got my glimpse of God working and moving me toward the Olympics, but I spent a lot more time thinking about the idea of hearts over medals. After my victory, I sat in the same room with this rider as we waited to be drug tested. I had a genuine moment on the inside where God directly asked me the question of what was more valuable: one heart or gold? As much as I wanted to win in London, I knew the answer. I didn't understand why my path kept crossing with her in such dramatic ways, but it did, and I wondered what God was trying to do. It put an exclamation point on the main message of the 2011 season, and confirmed that my challenge moving forward would be a very conscious requirement to stand firm because the spiritual battles were real.

From France, I returned home for a short break and then started training for 2012. And of course, things did not go perfectly. First, I struggled with a minor foot injury that turned out to be a blessing, because it changed the design of my training and held me back in a positive way. Then, because my digestive tract was doing strange things, I was often inconsistent or unpredictable with my performances. But always, when I really needed a dose of encouragement, there were glimpses of greatness on the bike reminding me that God still had me in His loving hands.

It wasn't about my training or the perfect plan. It was about Him and His doing. Not me. Not my husband. Not my coach. Consequently, I was forced to abide in the vine, trust God, and leave the consequences to Him. The subtle distractions and frustrations were simply attempts by the enemy to divert my focus.

But as long as I was abiding in Christ, I wouldn't get anxious or feel worried about the future. Instead, when things didn't go right and I battled these frequent minor obstacles, I still had a peace and calmness in the midst of the chaos.

In February, the 2012 racing season kicked off in Argentina with the Pan American Championships,[7] followed by a Tour in El Salvador. After the winter struggles, when I needed a reminder that I was on track, God blessed me with important early victories. I won the Pan American Championship Time Trial. I also went on to win two stages in El Salvador, and if it wasn't for a massive pothole breaking my bike, I would have won the overall title too.[8] It was an amazingly positive start to my season, but at the same time, it was still dotted with challenges. I was grateful to God for orchestrating with His foolishness to get me to where I needed to be—and then helping me stand firm in the midst of these obstacles.

Then, two races encapsulated the remainder of the "selection" season: the Chrono Gatineau in Canada and The Exergy Tour Time Trial stage. Both would have serious implications for selection to the Olympics, while giving God another moment to burn away any of my own desires that were still remaining. It was very similar to Joshua's defeat and subsequent victory at Ai in the Old Testament.

Joshua and Israel had come off a major victory at Jericho and wanted to go fight Ai. They thought they were ready and had a great plan, and they were confident. But they lost, and the defeat left Joshua and the people distraught and fearful. They thought God had given them the land, so what had gone wrong? There was confusion and dismay.

In defeat, though, God taught two valuable lessons. First, Joshua had to deal with the sin in the Israelite's own camp. Second, Joshua realized he had not inquired of the LORD before going forward. They were reminded that God wanted their whole-hearted obedience, and that it was always best to inquire of God first—and then only go when he said go.

However, in the midst of Joshua's confusion and discouragement, God also spoke to him. God knew he needed a word of encouragement and instruction, and He gave it. God helped Joshua stand firm *through* His word.

---

7. The Pan American Champion had an automatic start spot at World's, too. Yay.

8. The El Salvador trip is a book in itself. Somewhere on the internet there is a blog.

My Ai defeat was a one-day time trial in Canada. It was a big target for me, and my preparation for it was perfect. Up to this point, I had been riding well, abiding well, and navigating the people issues that arose as I stood for Christ in an environment that was not friendly to Him. I arrived in Ottawa, Canada, confident that I would win. But I didn't. I wasn't even good enough to be second. Instead, I lost the race and the head-to-head battle with another American rider, which compromised my fight for the Olympic TT.

Although it was just a race, it was my life, and I felt completely broken and confused. I honestly thought I had lost my chance to achieve my dream; a dream that I thought God had given me. When I didn't win that day, I thought God was saying no. I was dismayed, because I had been through so much, and yet until now, God was always working and moving me toward the goal. This result made me question myself and whether I was really in God's will in pursuing the Olympics. I was also bummed and broken, because I wanted the Games and the chance for gold so badly. In my defeat, I thought it was over, and I was crushed.

Through the night I cried, but instead of turning *from* God, I turned *toward* Him. I stood firm. I abided. I prayed and was in the Word. And as I did this honestly, with nothing to hide, He spoke, and I wrestled with my own heart. I thought I had surrendered enough times over the course of my journey, but had I completely? I wondered if it was possible that this sadness and brokenness was exactly where He wanted me. Emptied. Broken. Crushed. Confused. He finally had me at a point where I understood what 100-percent surrender was—and now I had to answer the question. As I did, I pondered whether I was more useful to Him in defeat and brokenness than I was in victory. As I lost, struggled, and experienced the adversities of life, He kept cracking my vessel ("pot")—and with each new crack, more of Him could escape through me. I started to accept that maybe He could do more this way, and I had to be okay with these methods. His kingdom was the goal. I knew this, but being able to surrender wholeheartedly that night was a true test of my motives, and it was hard. It hurt.

But as I let His Word speak to me, I was strengthened: *Do not be afraid, nor be dismayed (Joshua 1:9 NKJV). Rejoice in the Lord always...The Lord is near. Do not be anxious about anything, but in every situation, by prayer and petition, with thanksgiving, present your requests to God. And the peace of God, which transcends all understanding, will guard your hearts and your minds in Christ Jesus (Philippians 4:5-7). Lean not on your own understanding (Proverbs 3:5b).* I was…*hard pressed on every side, but not crushed; perplexed, but not in despair (2 Corinthians 4:8).* My ability to stand firm was a direct result of my abiding in Christ and being in His word, so that He could speak to me. Eventually, very late into the night, I let go, I trusted, and I determined to wait and listen.

Then about a week later, I actually had another chance. There was still the time trial stage at the Exergy Tour, and the more I thought about it, the more I realized that a win there was more important. My eyes were opened, and my heart was ready this time. I won the battle in prayer first, too, and I went when God said go. It was my Ai victory.

It was so incredible how the race played out. The course was not ideal for me, and we raced in a freezing rain, which was the worst case scenario for my small build. I was also in a situation where some individuals within the team hoped I would fail again, and I knew this. It was the ultimate pressure cooker, but I kept my blinders on, and focused only on Christ.

I was in a special zone of calmness and focus. I knew what I needed to do,

SELECTION

For every World Championship or Olympic Games, USA Cycling (the governing body of the sport of cycling in America), creates its own methods of selecting a team. Inherent in the process, is a gray area in how the criteria are written, or in how the team is chosen when there are discretionary spots left after the automatic positions (based on criteria) have been filled. As a result, selection often comes down to a decision where an individual or a group of individuals on a committee take into account all of the bubble athletes' results and history and then discuss each athletes' medal capability or their ability to impact team performance. In this case, multiple athletes can make an argument for the team, and it is a difficult decision for the selectors.

and I knew who was fighting for me that day. I went out and crushed the race and took the leader's jersey, too! Once again, God's foolishness was wiser than man's wisdom as he used me in spite of the conditions and my weaknesses.

A few weeks later, in the middle of June, the 2012 USA Olympic Road Cycling team was announced. I was named to my second Olympic team, and this time I would get to race the time trial! I melted in my room as I read the email. I thanked God for every detail of the journey; for His mercies, love, and strength, and I really let go again. I asked that He continue to shine through my cracks and help me continue to abide in Christ, so I could stand firm.

After all, my job was simply to abide in Christ so that His Spirit would enable me to do everything He was asking. IF I abided, THEN He could work and produce fruit in my life that would enable me to stand firm and could also potentially change the trajectory of others' lives. How cool was that?

CHAPTER 14

THE 2012 SUMMER OLYMPICS
The Games of the XXX Olympiad

Isaiah 64:4
Since ancient times no one has heard, no ear has perceived, no eye has seen any God besides you, who acts on behalf of those who wait for him.

1 Corinthians 1:25
For the foolishness of God is wiser than human wisdom, and the weakness of God is stronger than human strength.

WOOHOO!!!!!! I was officially a two-time USA Olympian in the sport of road cycling, and I was beyond excited, blessed, and motivated to see what God planned for the London Games. I expected big things. All of the puzzle pieces seemed to be in place. From my perspective, the timing was right, and my dream looked reachable. I was ready, and there were no limits with God! But I still had six and a half weeks to wait, which left Him plenty of time to hammer into me the necessity to chase the medal while not forgetting the greater, eternal purpose that surpassed everything. *Only then* would it be time to compete in one of the greatest spectacles of sport.

In the aftermath of being named to the team, I flew to Augusta, Georgia, to race the National Championships Time Trial and Road Race. My goal was to win the TT. The same one I had set for 10 years, but I had yet to achieve.

It only took 10 tries over 12 years, and it included seven 2nd place finishes and one 3rd. But when I least expected it, I finally won that elusive National Championship gold medal. Talk about patiently waiting and persevering for a goal! The victory encouraged me as I entered the final two weeks before the Olympics, and the pursuit of the ultimate gold medal I had been pursuing for the length of my career.

From Nationals, after a quick stop home, I flew to Germany for the Thüringen Rundfahrt—a seven-day race that would finish 10 days before my first event at the Olympics. It would finalize my preparation in two ways. First, the race would stress my body sufficiently while leaving me the right amount of time to recover and fine-tune my legs. Second, it allowed for a divinely orchestrated meeting and an unforgettable conversation with a fellow cyclist named Rachel in the backseat of a car on our drive to the Berlin airport.

It was a meeting that almost didn't happen. After the last stage, both of us needed to get to the airport. The German driver, who was her teammate, and the driver's friend, who was my teammate, had separately promised us rides without realizing how much stuff I had. The car was small, and it looked like it was going to be impossible to fit all four of us, my two bikes, and each of our bags into the vehicle. However, as I was preparing a separate ride, the German duo managed to pack the vehicle like sardines in a tin can. Then, Rachel and I weaved ourselves into the backseat between the bags. There was absolutely no more space left, but we did it! (By the way, THAT is the glamorous lifestyle I live!)

As we drove, Rachel and I talked. It had been a long time since I had seen her. She had been away from racing with various injuries and was now getting back into it. At first, the topics were small things, including the Olympics, but eventually a simple question about how she was doing exposed her brokenness, and the conversation shifted. The floodgates within her were free to open, and I was right where God needed me to be. As I shared about how I had survived my own adversity by standing on my ROCK (Christ), God was connecting with her heart and drawing her back to the faith and the relationship she had drifted from.

While I sat on the airplane on my short flight to London from Berlin, I marveled at how God operates. How He had worked in me, how He had used everything I had been through to equip me for that moment, and lastly, how He had actually trapped the two of us in that car together. It was a conversation with one person, but it tied together everything I had been through and everything I was trying to do within God's big-picture plans.

It was a unique, God-style sendoff to the Games. He used me in her life, but He also used her in mine to directly remind me there were hearts that He *could* reach through me. This idea of hearts over medals was legit, and God *could use* even me. I was humbled. I was just a vanilla bike racer, and there really was nothing super special about me, but it was true. God could do the extraordinary with the ordinary, when the ordinary (in their mission field of life) were available to Him.

Late on that July 22, I landed in London further motivated to win gold. I had two chances—the road race and the time trial. I didn't think it was possible to be more driven, but the potential platform was huge, and I was convinced the timing was right for God to use it. Winning a medal was also very realistic based on my history and recent results. Although I wasn't a favorite in the time trial, I was certainly on the list of contenders. Then, in the road race, we were one of the strongest teams, and I was willing and wanted to be a support player that helped Team USA win a medal.

Finally, it was July 29 and time to go for gold in the Road Race! As we drove in to The Mall in Central London where the race would start and finish, we could already see the crowds gathered in the stands and along the roads. Their enthusiasm and energy was palpable. Meanwhile, our excitement continued to escalate even further as we walked into the backstage area and tried to find our Team USA tent. There were masses of media, riders from all countries, support staff for each team, and official workers everywhere. This was the Olympic Games, *everyone* knew it, and there was a buzz and anticipation growing behind the scenes as much as there was in front.

There was still about an hour before the start, and I wanted to ride my bike for a few minutes while I had the chance. I typically like to warm up, but in this situation, warming up was not really possible or necessary. Instead, I was more interested in getting on my bike so that I could go out into the controlled chaos and craziness and immerse myself in the scene that was the London Olympic Games.

As I rolled slowly out onto the road between the stands and barricades, people began to recognize that I was an athlete, and the chants of U-S-A started everywhere! There were cheers for me from people I did not know but who knew me, and cheers from Americans who were not cycling fans per se but were there to support Team USA at the Olympic Games. It was so amazing. And in the middle of it all, I heard my husband's voice! I looked up and spotted him in the front row with a giant sign that said, "GO AMBER!" I immediately rode over to give him a kiss and a chance to share the moment. Right there, the emotion and magnitude of my own journey and his love hit me with a strength that required me to hold back the tears.

After our brief encounter, I continued to ride slowly out the first two kilometers of the race course before returning back to the start boxes. All the way out and back, I heard so many cheers and USA chants. I saw countless numbers of smiles, flags and people from all different nations. The masses of people and their energy were so different than Beijing. I was happy I had taken a moment to breathe it all in before the focus of the race took over.

Just before it was time to start, my teammates and I walked out onto a special stage set up in the middle of the road where we could sign our names in a box denoted by our race number on a transparent wall behind us. This was the official "sign-in" for the race. After we signed, we posed for a team photo as the video coverage plastered us onto the giant TV screens all over London. It was a cool moment. The stands of spectators were on both sides, the giant sign-in board was behind us, and the throngs of photographers and cameramen from all over the world were piled down in front. We were USA's Olympic Team, and it was almost our game time.

The day before, we had planned our strategy. Shelley Olds was our sprinter (and my roommate in the village) who had proven over the recent years that she would be ready, both physically and mentally, and could be counted on. She was capable of winning from a break or a big group, and she could climb. The course actually suited her strengths, and I could see it in her eyes, so I expected big things from her. Then, we had Evelyn "Evie" Stevens who was less experienced, but very strong and capable of breaking away for the win. We would take our chances with her if it worked that way. Finally, Kristin Armstrong was a multiple world champion and already a gold medalist from the Beijing Olympics four years prior. The time trial was her primary goal, but she could never be discounted. Her strength and her will were second to none. And then there was me, and I just wanted the team to win a medal. I was willing to do everything I could to make it happen. I knew that if the team was going to succeed, someone needed to play the early worker role. My experience had taught me how important this was, and I would do it. We were one of the strongest teams in the world, but only if we rode as a unit.

After the sign-in, we staged on the start line. Now it was time to show our strength. The gun fired, and the bunch of riders rolled out of the London Mall and through the city streets together. I dropped to the back of the group where I aimed to conserve my energy by not getting caught up in the nervousness of the bunch. Once this subsided, and just prior to the attacks, I moved back to the front where I could see the race well and actively do my job.

As we rode through London and into Surrey County, I observed the spectators were not just at the start and finish. There were communities of people—British, Dutch, German, American, etc.,—stacked up behind the barricades covering the entire course. The sheer number of people and the volume and intensity of the cheering was one of the most incredible things I have ever experienced. It followed us around for 140 kilometers. And even when we returned back through London, they were still there and as loud as ever despite the skies unloading torrents of rain on them.

The race itself went almost perfectly. I had fun, and I was feeling very good. I wanted to keep the USA in an offensive position, so I followed or jumped to every split or break attempt that was dangerous. I was easily seeing and reading the race, and it wasn't my job to conserve for the finish, so I rode hard.

Then, on the Box Hill circuits, the hardest part of the race, there were multiple times where I was able to go with, or create, a break. I was still smiling and racing hard, and I could sense the rubber band was about to snap where I had predicted it would. And when it did, Shelley Olds was one of four riders in what would become the winning break. It was a great situation for us. She was faster than all but one rider and was a lock for the silver. But since she was also riding smart and conserving in the breakaway, it was very possible that she could have been gold.

But then, "bike racing" happened to her, and she punctured a tire. When I saw her on the side of the road, my heart broke for her. I waited to help her get back into the peloton, but the race for a medal was essentially over. Her opportunity was lost because that breakaway, which should have had her in it, stayed away to the finish line.

As the rest of the peloton screamed back into town while chasing those three riders who were still off, there were crashes everywhere. It was still pouring rain, and the roads were slick. It was clear the other riders were not going be caught, so as we entered the final two kilometers, I let the peloton go ahead. I was empty. My legs were completely finished, and my job was done. I did not need to fight for 20th place. Instead, I soaked in the sights and sounds of the long finish straight. It was an epic day. We had raced well as a team, but we had nothing to show for it. I was soaking wet, cold, and disappointed for our team, but not as disappointed as Shelley. She was the one who lost a medal, and I was bummed for her.

But the Games weren't over. After a day of rest and recovery, and then a day to regenerate and dial in my body and mind, I was ready to go hard again. It was finally time to race the Time Trial in the Olympic Games. I was a little nervous, but mostly I felt ready. I had waited since 2004 to do this. I was very prepared and confident. I knew my form was good based on how I felt and rode in the Road Race, and my eyes were still firmly fixed on Christ.

I had surrendered my dream to Him, and I was anxiously waiting for what He would do next. I asked for His strength and focus to do my best, and that I might honor Him in victory or defeat. I knew His plans were bigger and better than anything I could imagine or understand. I wanted to win, but I trusted His love, and I let go.

Two hours before my race, I put on my quiet music and went into my focus zone. Then with this peaceful mindset, I left the hotel by bike to ride the course very easily. This provided my body with a slow, gentle warm up while it also allowed me to make my final observations on the wind.

An hour before my start time, I got on the trainer and started my official warm-up. It was time to take my body to new places, and I needed to go just hard enough on the trainer to turn on all of my physiological systems. I finished the warm-up about 20 minutes prior to my start. I made a quick trip to the port-a-pot, pulled up my skinsuit, put on my helmet and glasses, and rode my race bike over to the start house.

As each final minute passed, the intensity ratcheted up. But as it did, I continued to find myself in the zone of amped up calmness in the midst of the chaos. I was ready. My butterflies were out of their waiting room and flying in perfect formation, providing just a touch of nervous excitement. Enough to tell me I was prepared, but not too much to take away from my performance.

At the 90-second mark, I climbed onto the start ramp and handed my bike to the man in charge of holding it in place for me. With 60 seconds left, I got on the bike as he held it steady. I looked ahead to the first corner. The crowds on each side were a blur, and the noise slowly went away, while the task at hand was crystal clear. I took one last deep belly breath at 10 seconds, gripped my handlebars, and prepared to step down hard. Three seconds, two, one, GO. I was out of the gate and onto the course.

Before I knew it, I had reached the first time check. There had been a wave of energy from the crowds following me, so even though I was riding hard, I barely felt the sensations of pain from my effort as the intensity in the atmosphere carried me. I felt like I had great rhythm, I was pacing well, and I thought I was having the special day I expected. I was in the moment of every pedal stroke. My mind was completely focused, and I continued to push all of the way around the course. As I neared the finish line, I sprinted with everything I had left. What a race! I was on the hot seat.

But as quickly as I climbed into the queen's chair, I had to leave it. Rider after rider passed me, and I ended up being 7th place. I was disappointed with the result. I believed that on my best day, I was capable. It was definitely in me.

However, that day I was only really good, and I needed to be great. Winning on the biggest day of the biggest stage required me to be nearly perfect, and I wasn't that day. That's just the hard truth of the sport.

However, at the same time, I wasn't disappointed with my effort. I had given everything I had, and I had no regrets. None. My preparation was great, my focus was dialed, and my rhythm was right. I had done my best *that* day.

As I thought about the finality of the race, I changed my clothes and made my way out of the secure area and over to the American corner near the start line. I found my husband and gave him a big, teary hug. I was fine, because I knew God had me. I knew He would do greater things with this, but there was still a lifetime's worth of emotion tied to the loss, and I felt it.

It was a huge goal, and I was so close, but I did not achieve it. At least I did not achieve the earthly medal. However, through the entire process, I had seen God working. And as I grew to take on His perspective, I also understood how the eternal outweighed the temporary. And if, through that process of going for gold but missing it, even one life was impacted, then it was worth it. I did not get what I wanted in the short term, but God did what was best in the long term. His ways are not our ways, and that's okay with me. He is God. But I also knew He loved me enough to die for me, and although I did not always understand or agree, I knew He wanted the best. I trusted Him in the *right now* and let Him work in me and through me.

About seven weeks later, I competed at the 2012 World Championships. My team won the Team Time Trial World Championship, I struggled in the individual Time Trial again, but then I went on to earn 4th place (and the wood medal) in the World Championship Road Race.

Normally, 4th is the worst place to be, but my real medal was in the break with me. At the finish line, Rachel gave me the biggest hug, and I felt God's love in it. There it was…the heart and the medal (Rachel was 2nd) in the same place. It was beautiful, and for once, I could smile with a 4th place finish.

What a year! I was the 2012 Pan Am Champion, National Champion, an Olympian, a TTT World Champion, and a 4th place finisher in the World Championship Road Race. Although I considered retiring, 2013 beckoned. God was still working. I was tired, but He said press on…again. So I did, still expecting to do great things.

CHAPTER 15

WHEN SHMACK HAPPENS

The Post Script

Psalm 46:10
Be still, and know that I am God;

2 Corinthians 12:9
My grace is sufficient for you...

Psalm 62:1-2, 8
Truly my soul silently waits for God; From Him comes my salvation. He only is my rock and my salvation; He is my defense; I shall not be greatly moved. Trust in Him at all times, you people; Pour out your heart before Him; God is a refuge for us. (NKJV)

A fter all of the athletic success and spiritual development that had taken place over the course of my life and career, I entered 2013 poised for God to do something spectacular for His kingdom purposes. The story He had written with me was powerful, and there was potential for Him to inspire and encourage through it. I was hopeful. But just as quickly as it started, the road I expected to be walking was not the one I was on. The winter and spring were both disappointing and challenging, and then things went from bad to worse on May 17 at the Tour of California Time Trial. The SHMACK happened, and I found myself physically battered and broken.

I had hit the wall, literally. But through the entire ordeal—as I lay on the pavement waiting for medical help to arrive, as the ambulance transported me, and as the trauma center events unfolded—I was filled with a peace and a strength that was beyond me. I had what I needed exactly when I needed it through Christ. He did not forsake me. He was my rock and my refuge—and although the storm pounded me, I stood still. And I could, because I knew Him.

This continued as I rehabbed the damage it left behind: My body was messed up. So for the short term, I needed to set a new reference point for my mind to be able to gauge my progress. I used my first hours lying in pain in the hospital as my "pavement" zero marker. Then from a rehabilitation perspective, I would only improve with each minute, hour, and day moving forward, and I could leave the trauma behind me. It had happened, and there were no do-overs. I accepted where I was, and I controlled my attitude and my focus going forward.

Instead of thinking about everything I *could not* do, I intentionally only focused on those things I *could* do, and I continued to reference 'pavement zero.' The first night, I was able to stand up on crutches, something impossible 10 hours earlier. That was good. I was healing. Then, because of my broken ribs and my body's desire to breathe shallowly, the doctor recommended that I take 10 deep breaths every hour to prevent pneumonia from setting in. Again, that was one more thing I could do, so every time I thought about it through the night, I breathed!

Then, the next day, I could do a little more. Mostly I was in a wheelchair, but I did manage to take a few, slow steps with my crutches. It was still difficult to do everything, so I rested, I breathed, and I stayed still before God. With each day, though, I could take a few more steps, and I could do a little more. Healthy muscles that had turned off to protect me were turning back on, the wounds were healing, and the inflammation and bruising were moving through their own stages. I was healing.

Soon, I was sitting on a recumbent bike at Rausch Physical Therapy, where I could use the pedals to force my legs to move gently. It was tedious. I didn't even register 1mph, but I moved. Days later, I made it up to 3-4mph. And slowly, I improved so that I could walk with one crutch, I could pedal faster and with more force, I could sit down and stand up on my own, and I could eventually walk without a crutch. I even rode my own bike, easily, on a stationary trainer! The doctors and the PT's trusted me to listen to my body whisper or talk, so I let it guide my recovery. As I pushed it in an intelligent way, it responded. It took time, though, and I had to patiently work through the process.

During my weeks and months of physical rehabilitation, I also paid attention to the details. I kept my diet very clean and fed my body the most important and highest quality nutrients. It was working exhaustively to fix itself, so I did not neglect this aspect of my recovery. I used the tools that I had available to me through my physical therapy office: the Laser and the Alter G. I also used Podium Legs to help increase the blood flow to my legs while pushing out the fluid. Then, my soft tissue specialists, Cynthia and Melissa, worked carefully where they could.

Every day my therapists were in awe of my progress, because my body was healing so fast. I was too. I have no doubt that God heard the countless prayers that so many people lifted up on my behalf. I was truly a miracle in how fast I recovered. It helped that I was in great shape and so mentally tough, but there was an element of it all that was beyond me, and I am not afraid to say it. I lived it!

Through it all, I continued to hear the Lord speaking Psalm 46:10 to me: *Amber, BE STILL and KNOW that I am God. Turn from the obstacle and see me. There is opportunity if you wait on me, if you rest in me, if you are still and let me work.* It is normally very hard for me to stop and do nothing, but for the first time in my life, I didn't struggle with this. I knew God was going to do something special. Actually, He was already doing something special.

My faith had been developed and strengthened up to this point, and because I had been in the Word enough to know God and how He works, it was easy for me to take refuge in Him and wait this time. The latest storm had blasted me, but my ROCK did not move or change, and the tighter I held on, the more He responded to me. Then, as I was still, eventually His voice became clear too.

I heard, "Go build an Ark!" Well, actually, I heard, "Write a book. Write the story that I have written into your life." But for me, writing a book seemed almost as far-fetched as building an ark. However, just as Noah knew God's voice, knew he needed to obey, and believed God would equip him to get it done, I clearly heard God say *write*, and I knew not to underestimate Him. I also understood that as I depended on Him and surrendered my will to Him, I needed to be diligent in taking care of my responsibilities. As I healed, I couldn't ride, but I could write! I didn't know what would happen after, but for now I would write and trust that God would part the seas as I stepped in faith.

My story is unique to me, but having to face adversity is universal. It is guaranteed in some form. Fear, discouragement, sickness, brokenness, pain, being hurt by people we trust, the countless direct and indirect attacks from the enemy, wanting to do or achieve something but being told to wait by God, being refined and molded, or even hitting the wall in some literal or metaphorical way is all part of life.

How that stuff happens is specific to each of us, but how we can conquer it is the same. Our God is the same. The same tools that Joshua, Abraham, and Paul used, I used. You can use. The same God that delivered Daniel delivered me. The same grace is sufficient, the same power is perfected in our weaknesses, and the same peace is readily available. And THE ROCK I cling to is beyond big enough for all of us to cling to.

True, it is easy to say and do it now, because my faith is strong. However, it developed in steps just like my Olympic and World Championship achievements did. The initial foundation was laid, and then the end result came after building year after year on what I had done previously. There was not an "easy" button. The progression took time, and it required perseverance and patience, and the perspective to see the big picture of where I was going.

It wasn't pretty at first. When I first entered the cycling world, I wore underwear under my bike shorts, I was unsure of how to use the toe clips, and of all things, I raced in a T-Shirt! I didn't know any better, but I still tried. Then I researched, I listened to wise counsel, I learned, and I grew to be an expert in my field. The same is true with our faith. God starts with us exactly as we are and then gets us to where we want to be through a *process*.

My abilities to trust God with all my heart, gain His perspective, endure, be courageous, be fearless and stand firm—all during the process of being transformed into Christ's likeness—have improved over time through the pressures, squalls, and hurricanes of life. The principle of overload has applied to my faith as much as it has applied to my athletic life. There would have never been development and growth without the increased stress and pressure. As uncomfortable as I might have been in the short term, the long term value has been priceless.

Even being able to walk in the Spirit has been a step-by-step process. As soon as I became a Christian, I was filled with the Spirit, but I have had to learn to walk in Him like a baby learns to walk, through trial and error; one step at a time. Neither the baby nor I were born ready to run a marathon, and thankfully, we didn't need to. We just had to step.

Most importantly, through everything, I have gotten to know Jesus. I don't simply know about Jesus. I know Jesus. I have a ROCK to stand on, cling to, and take refuge under. His peace and strength are real. I have seen His faithfulness daily. And His grace IS sufficient…and AMAZING.

I'm not sure what's next from a riding perspective. As you can imagine, my last accident makes it very easy to want to stop. However, I think I may be like Peter that night he came back from fishing empty-handed. Peter, the pro fisherman, knew there was nothing left to do, but Jesus, the God of the universe, told him to go back out.[1] Like Peter, I am tired and ready to be finished. I feel like I have done enough, but I think Jesus is telling me to go back out one more time. Peter obeyed, and that set the stage for His future as a fisher of men. Perhaps, if I obey, Jesus will send me out, and I will return with a net full of fish, too.

---

1. Luke 5:4-5.

Right now, I am praying for discernment for the next step, how to do it, and how far ahead to look. If I need to 'go back out' one more time, what does that mean? Is it one more race, one more season or do I really consider an attempt at another Olympic Games? It seems impossible, but that is the business of our God. As I inquire of Him and do my best to wait and listen, I will be diligent on my end. I know He will open or close doors and direct my steps.

I have had fun writing about how God's truths have applied to me in the context of who God made me and where He placed me, and how those truths have allowed me to endure and win. In the grand scheme of life, I know my trials and tribulations have not been that bad, but they were still storms. And the truth is that adversity in some form is a part of every race, so we all need the same God. Life's challenges are specific to each of us, but the tools required to respond, embrace, and overcome are exactly the same.

I pray that you can see how awesome God is and how timeless His words are and apply them in your own life. I pray that instead of *giving* up, you *get* up one more time. That you turn to God and not away from Him, and you allow Him to work through the adversity. And in it, you taste his strength. God wants to make us all champions. Whether we are athletes, business people, parents, teachers, doctors, trash collectors, or whatever the call, God is always working in us and through us...even *when SHMACK happens*. Nobody is too small or insignificant to receive His love or do great things for Him.

EPILOGUE

"Another year is approaching, full of promise and boasting of new dreams. The faith and hope I find in Christ that has carried me this far, continues to grow deeper still. And with the 2016 Olympics just a few short seasons away, something is beginning to stir in my heart. My body is well, my heart is tuned in to how God desires to direct my steps, and the thought of *one more time* is on my mind. One more time." Follow my unfolding journey at: www.amberneben.com.

AFTERWORD

My Debt and my Mediator

The trauma bills have rolled in from every angle since the SHMACK in May 2013; the ambulance ride, the ambulance staff, the trauma, the emergency physicians, the imaging, the follow-up doctors, X-rays and CT's, and the physical therapy. Before any insurance processing, the trauma center bill alone was almost $70,000. I was only there for eight hours, and it cost me much more than my annual salary! Even after the race insurance coverage kicked in, I was still left with 30 percent of the bill after I pay a $5,000 deductible. Not only did the accident hurt, but it cost a lot, too. Of course insurance helps, but I still must pay my part. Thankfully, I have something better in life. On the cross before Jesus breathed His last words, He cried out, "Tetelestai." Translated, this means 'Paid in full' or 'It is finished.' It signified that nothing else needed to be added, and God's redemption plan was now complete. Jesus substituted himself for me (us,) and my (our) sin debt was paid in full with that act of love. Then, He completed the victory with His resurrection.

Through Christ, my eternal life is guaranteed, and I have a hope and a peace that transcends the temporary troubles of this world. The moment I confessed that I was a sinner (that I missed the mark of perfection), and I accepted Christ as my God and Savior, my old self died, and I was born again in Christ. I became a new creation on the inside, an adopted child of God with full rights, and I was filled with the Holy Spirit through whom I am strengthened and enabled to do everything I described in this book. My sins were forgiven and forgotten. The guilt is gone, the love is real, and the relationship is growing. But most importantly, my room in the House of the Lord is booked FOREVER.

…all because of Jesus.

Will you make that same confession and receive the same gift of salvation? The challenge is to know Jesus. Not the counterfeits, but the Christ of the Bible—the living God of the universe. He is waiting for a response. He wants to put His arms around you and carry you through this life and take you with Him into the next.

It's not complicated. It's just Jesus. Nothing more. Nothing less. Come as you are.

John 3:16-18

For God so loved the world that he gave his one and only Son, that whoever believes in him shall not perish but have eternal life. For God did not send his Son into the world to condemn the world, but to save the world through him. Whoever believes in him is not condemned, but whoever does not believe stands condemned already because they have not believed in the name of God's one and only Son..

Romans 1:19-20

since what may be known about God is plain to them, because God has made it plain to them. For since the creation of the world God's invisible qualities—his eternal power and divine nature—have been clearly seen, being understood from what has been made, so that people are without excuse.

Romans 3:23

for all have sinned and fall short of the glory of God,

Romans 5:8

But God demonstrates his own love for us in this: While we were still sinners, Christ died for us.

Romans 6:23

For the wages of sin is death, but the gift of God is eternal life in Christ Jesus our Lord.

Romans 10:9-11

If you declare with your mouth, "Jesus is Lord," and believe in your heart that God raised him from the dead, you will be saved. For it is with your heart that you believe and are justified, and it is with your mouth that you profess your faith and are saved. As Scripture says, "Anyone who believes in him will never be put to shame."

Romans 12:1-2

Therefore, I urge you, brothers and sisters, in view of God's mercy, to offer your bodies as a living sacrifice, holy and pleasing to God—this is your true and proper worship. Do not conform to the pattern of this world, but be transformed by the renewing of your mind. Then you will be able to test and approve what God's will is—his good, pleasing and perfect will.

ROAD RACING 101

Just as its name implies, the discipline of road cycling takes place on paved roadways. Considered to be the most traditional and popular form of bike racing, road cycling takes on many different forms. Cycling events contested on the road include time trials, road races, stage races, criteriums, omniums, team time trials, and circuit races. The Olympic Games feature two of these events: road race and time trial.

Road Races

Road races are team-oriented, mass-start events which typically feature a field of 150-180 riders. Teams are generally made up of eight to 10 riders, except at the Olympic Games where team sizes are limited to a maximum of five for men and four for women.

Road races generally take place on public roads and can be point-to-point races or multiple circuits of a loop anywhere from 5 to 25 miles in length.

During a road race, team members work together to gain an advantage over other riders, usually designating one person as team leader. The team leader is determined prior to the race and can be based on several factors including the course's terrain, a rider's fitness level, and the competition. The leader's teammates will help in any way possible from fetching food and water to giving up a wheel or their bicycle in the event of a crash or mechanical failure. Throughout most of the race, a team's leader will ride in the draft of a teammate, never facing the wind head-on unless absolutely necessary.

Behind the peloton, a caravan follows the race. The caravan typically consists of race officials, team cars, media and VIP cars, neutral support vehicles, and medical personnel. Each team is allowed one car per caravan in which the team director sits and advises his athletes. A team mechanic also sits in the caravan car, ready to service a rider with equipment if he or she suffers a flat tire, a crash, or any other mechanical failure.

Individual Time Trials

Often called "The Race of Truth," the time trial pits individuals against the clock instead of against each other. It's the most basic form of competitive cycling and the rules are simple: the athlete with the fastest time over a given distance is the winner.

Like road races, the time trial usually takes place on public roads and can be a point-to-point race or multiple laps of a circuit.

In a race against the clock, results are often determined by fractions of a second. And since there are no team tactics and riders don't have the benefit of drafting off each other, riders seek out every aerodynamic advantage they can. The time trial features the most technologically-advanced equipment such as carbon fiber disc wheels, lightweight components, teardrop-shaped aerodynamic helmets, one-piece skinsuits, and special handlebars which allow a rider to get into a more aerodynamic position.

Riders start one-by-one at specific intervals, usually one minute, by descending down a small start ramp onto the course.

Stage Races

Stage races are multi-day races that string together several stages. The rider with the lowest cumulative time after all stages are complete is declared the winner. The most popular example of a stage race is the Tour de France – a 21-day race every July that is considered to be the most prestigious competitive cycling event in the world.

This grueling combination of events, which can be as short as two days or as long as three weeks, usually incorporates both road races and time trials. A small local stage race might include a time trial on Saturday and a road race on Sunday. The Tour de France typically includes a time trial prologue plus 20 other road race and time trial stages.

Following each day's competition a leader's jersey (usually yellow in color) is awarded to the rider with the lowest cumulative time to designate the current leader of the race.

Because time trials and mountain stages are typically the deciding factors in major stage races, riders who excel at those two specialties are often times considered major contenders for overall victories in stage races. For riders who aren't all-around specialists, strong climbers, or strong time trialists, an individual stage win is also considered a prestigious accomplishment.

In addition to the overall winner, most stage races also incorporate other competitions and award jerseys to the best sprinter, best climber, best young rider, most aggressive rider, and the best team.

Because the overall winner is determined solely by cumulative time, it's possible to win a stage race without actually winning an individual stage.

Criteriums

Although not an internationally-recognized discipline, criterium racing is purely American and one of the most common forms of competitive cycling in the United States. Designed for spectators, criteriums are races held on short circuits, typically in an urban setting.

These fast-paced events are usually 25-60 miles in length and last between one and two hours. The relatively short, closed course features several corners and gives spectators the opportunity to view most of the race. In criteriums, the pace is fast from the gun as riders can average up to 30 miles per hour for the duration of the race. Quick acceleration and keen bike handling skills are paramount to success.

These races often end in field sprints, and typically a sprinter with the fastest finishing kick will win. In a criterium, if a rider crashes, suffers a flat tire or other mechanical failure, he or she can enter the pit area where a team mechanic has one lap to make a quick repair. After the fix, the rider is reinserted into the same position he or she was before the mishap.

It is important for a rider to remain near the front of the peloton as the first few riders can take a corner with little or no braking. Those further back jockey for position into the turn, brake and then sprint to catch back up. The resulting "accordion" effect takes its toll on riders who navigate hundreds of turns throughout the course of a race.

Omniums

Omniums are similar to stage races but instead recognize an overall winner based on the accumulation of points instead of lowest cumulative time. Following each stage, a rider is awarded points corresponding to his of her stage finish. Following the completion of the last stage, the rider with the most points is declared the winner.

Circuit Races

The term "circuit race" is generally used to describe a race that covers several laps of a circuit that is more than a mile, but less than five miles. The course is longer than that of a criterium, but shorter than loops used in a road race.

Team Time Trials

Like the individual time trial, the team time trial is simply a race against the clock with teams racing one at a time and working together to complete the course in the fastest possible time. In a team time trial, the science of drafting plays a major role as teammates take turns at the front of the paceline. When a rider "takes a pull," the rest of his or her teammates fall in behind and expend up to 30% less energy to achieve the same speed. When the lead rider is unable to maintain the same pace, he or she rotates to the back of the paceline as a "fresh" rider takes over the pacesetting.

Content provided by USA Cycling.

CYCLING TERMINOLOGY

Like most sports, competitive cycling utilizes a unique set of terminology. Whether it's road cycling, mountain biking, track racing or BMX, there are many terms one should be familiar with. Below is a list of the most common terms used throughout the sport of cycling.

Attack: A sudden attempt to get away from a rider or group of riders.

Bonk: When a rider completely runs out of energy.

Breakaway: A rider or group of riders who has separated themselves ahead of the main pack.

Bridge the Gap: When a rider or group of riders attempt to advance from a group of riders to one further ahead.

Caravan: The line of cars which typically follow a road race; includes team cars, race officials, media, medical, VIP and neutral support vehicles.

Chasers: Riders who are attempting to advance to a rider or group of riders ahead.

Chicane: A series of tight, technical turns.

Compact Crank: A crankset with smaller chain rings (50 teeth and 34 teeth). This helps make the gearing easier.

Crankset (diagram): The combination of the big ring, the small ring, and the crank arms where the pedals attach. The standard sized chain rings are 53 teeth and 39 teeth.

Criterium: A multi-lap road race on a course usually a mile or less in length.

Director Sportif: The traditional name for the team manager.

Drafting: Riding in the slipstream of another rider ahead. A rider drafting off another generally expends 30% less energy.

Drop: To leave another rider or group of riders behind by attacking.

Echelon: A line of riders positioned behind one another to receive maximum protection from the wind.

Endo: A crash which results in a rider going over the front handlebars.

Endurance Base Training: Training long hours in the comfortable aerobic heart rate zone.

Field: The main group of riders, also known as the Pack, Peloton or Bunch.

Field Sprint: The final sprint between the main group of riders in a race, not always for first place.

Jump: A sudden acceleration, often at the start of a sprint.

Peloton: The main group of riders during a road race.

Rear Cog Set (diagram): The gears on the rear wheel.

Sitting In: When one rider refuses to take a pull and break the wind for a group in which he's riding.